MISSIONS:
MINISTERING
BEYOND
OUR BORDERS

WHAT "MISSIONS" MEANS
FOR THE MISSIONARY

WALKING IN THE WORD
MINISTRIES

Missionary/Pastor Jeremy Markle
787-374-1034
jmarkle@baptistworldmission.org

Missions: Ministering Beyond Our Borders (Missionary Edition)
What "Missions" Means for the Missionary
by Missionary/Pastor Jeremy Markle

Unless otherwise noted, all Scripture quotations are from the King James Version.

Published by Walking in the WORD Ministries
787-374-1034
jmarkle@baptistworldmission.org

Printed in the United States of America

ISBN 978-0692303870

I wish to lovingly dedicate this book
to my wife, Laura,
who has faithfully joined me
in every aspect of my life and ministry.

I also wish to dedicate this book
to my three children,
Jeremiah, Juliana, and Joshua,
who are an integral part of our ministry
as my wife and I enjoy training them
for the glory of God.

Special Thank You

To PEP Writing Services for editing services and to Pastor Scott Markle and Joanna Lynch for help with graphic design and formatting.

CONTENTS

THE MISSIONARY'S COMFORT AND COUNSEL AS HE ADJUSTS TO HIS NEW LIFE AND MINISTRY

PREFACE

This book has been written to provide insight into the physical, emotional, and spiritual adjustments a missionary faces as he begins his new life and ministry. Throughout its pages you will find spiritual encouragements for the missionary and helpful hints for his family and friends who desire to support him in his service to their Lord and Savior Jesus Christ.

The "Letter to the Reader" expresses a personal caution for the reader to be open-minded and kind-hearted as he reads about the real struggles that missionaries encounter. It encourages the reader, whether missionary or missionary supporter, to be gracious as the physical and spiritual struggles of missions are openly illustrated and discussed with the goal of revealing Biblical comfort and counsel for each topic.

The "Introduction" encourages the reader to balance the physical and emotional realities of missionary work with the spiritual joy of harvesting God's reward.

Each chapter presents its subject matter by considering four progressive points of view of a missionary's life and circumstances: The Missionary Experience, The Biblical Example, The Actual Events, and The Biblical Exhortation.

"The Missionary Experience" provides a brief synopsis of what a missionary may experience as he pursues God's call for his life. This brief introduction to the subject matter is based on real experiences missionaries have faced and is provided as an explanation of the importance of the specific subject of that chapter.

"The Biblical Example" seeks to help the reader understand that his experiences are not new. They have been faced by others who have followed God's will for their lives and ministries throughout the Scriptures. By considering these examples, the missionary will have the opportunity to see examples of both correct and incorrect responses, as well as their results. It will also give the reader a 20/20 perspective of how God has used similar situations not to destroy His servants but rather to enhance their usability and bless their obedience in the end.

"The Actual Events" is an opportunity for the author to share his personal experience or those of fellow missionaries he knows in order to help the reader understand that he is not alone. It also provides the opportunity to present specific spiritual lessons learned as he or others he knows have experienced the subject first hand.

"The Biblical Exhortation" concludes the chapter by giving specific verses and passages of Scripture to direct the reader in the days and weeks that follow. The exhortation has a two-fold purpose: first, to provide the reader with clear Biblical instruction as to how he must follow God's Word and will in his life, and second, to provide a spiritual pep talk for those who are growing weary in the work.

As each chapter concludes, three extra resources are provided. First, practical advice is given for each of the three different participants in the ministry of missions: the missionary candidate, the missionary's supporters, and the missionary in service. Second, extra passages of Scripture are included to help build the faith of those missionaries who are facing the specific trial or situations that have been addressed. Third, extra examples of Biblical characters who faced similar circumstances is provided, along with the passage reference so that further Biblical study can be made.

The missionary's edition of the book includes an appendix that gives outlines and tips to help the missionary begin his new life and ministry on his field of service. Although each field of service is different, these outlines and tips are presented in such a way as to provide both detailed suggestions as well as general principles in directing the missionary to make wise choices in many of his tough decisions. The subject matter includes, but is not limited to, language learning, health concerns, housing arrangements, and church facilities.

The Missionary's Life,
A Life of Faith

Faith or Foolishness

Hebrews 11:1
*Now faith is the substance of things hoped for,
the evidence of things not seen.*

Faith is based on Facts
and produces Fidelity

Foolishness is based on Fiction
and produces Failure

Romans 10:17
*So then faith cometh by hearing,
and hearing by the word of God.*

Place your faith
in the truths of the Scriptures
and in the God that they reveal!

Hebrews 11:6
*But without faith it is impossible to please him:
for he that cometh to God must believe that he is,
and that he is a rewarder of them that diligently seek him.*

Letter to the Reader

CAUTION, HANDLE WITH CARE

Dear Friend,

As I begin sharing with you some of the often alluded to, but rarely specified nor properly prepared for, effects of "culture shock" and ministry pressure in the first years of a missionary's life and ministry on the foreign field, I find myself thinking of these words: "CAUTION, HANDLE WITH CARE." The subject on which we are about to embark is similar to much of the medication of our day. Medication can provide strength and healing; or, when applied incorrectly, it can destroy and even bring death. And so it is with the realities of missions.

*The Apostle Paul was concerned that his burdens in ministry for the believers in Ephesus would cause them to be discouraged and spiritually faint. For this reason he said, "**Wherefore I desire that ye faint not at my tribulations for you, which is your glory**" (Ephesians 3:13). He then continues by sharing his desired outcome for them, knowing about the realities of his ministry, as he reveals his prayer to God for them. "**For this cause I bow my knees unto the Father of our Lord Jesus Christ, Of whom the whole family in heaven and earth is named, That he would grant you, according to the riches of his glory, to be strengthened with might by his Spirit in the inner man; That Christ may dwell in your hearts by faith; that ye, being rooted and grounded in love, May be able to comprehend with all saints what is the breadth, and length, and depth, and height; And to know the love of Christ, which passeth knowledge, that ye might be filled with all the fulness of God**" (Ephesians 4:14-19). He finishes by sharing his confidence in the power of God to provide such awesome strength and the knowledge of His presence and love for the* them by saying, *"Now unto him that is able to do exceeding abundantly above all that we ask or think, according to the power that worketh in us, Unto him be glory in the church by Christ Jesus throughout all ages, world without end. Amen"* (Ephesians 3:20-21).

And so we come to the reason for taking time to honestly evaluate the many struggles which God's servants face as they follow His will in the life and work of missions. It is not that we become overwhelmed with fear and shrink back from the task at hand, nor that we wallow in self-pity, but that we find God's strength and presence on a daily basis to continue to accomplish His will for His Glory, and that we might pause to sincerely consider, personally prepare for, and readily come alongside others to uplift them as we all face these realities while sacrificially serving our King!. Our hearts must be awakened so that we are realistically alert to the level of dedication we must have to fulfill a life of discipleship. In the words of Jesus Christ, *"For which of you, intending to build a tower, sitteth not down first, and counteth the cost, whether he have sufficient to finish it? Lest haply, after he hath laid the foundation, and is not able to finish it, all that behold it begin to mock him, Saying, This man began to build, and was not able to finish"* (Luke 14:28-30). Believers must *"count the cost"*!

We cannot ignore nor cover up the true cost of being a disciple of Christ. We must personally accept and publicly teach to the present and future generations that *"ye [we] are not your [our] own? For ye [we] are bought with a price: therefore glorify God in your [our] body, and in your [our] spirit, which are God's"* (I Corinthians 6:19-20). Each believer must be willing to *"present your [their] bodies a living sacrifice, holy, acceptable unto God, which is your [their] reasonable service"* (Romans 12:1).

For many missionaries, the presenting of their physical body on the altar of martyrdom is a reality that may not be avoided and carries with it a sense of heroism. Many believers declare to Jesus, as Peter did, *"I will lay down my life for thy sake"* (John 13:37). But sadly, they also follow Peter's example of discouragement and ultimate desertion when they are not called upon to die but rather to live a life of death (death to personal ambitions, dreams, accomplishments, etc.).

In Romans 12:1 Paul was not asking for believers to be a dead sacrifice but rather a *"living sacrifice."* He was teaching a daily sacrifice of deliberate death to self while still living in this physical world. Paul proclaimed his dedication to this type of sacrifice by stating, *"I am crucified with Christ: nevertheless I live; yet not I, but Christ liveth in me: and the life which I now live in the flesh I live by the faith of the Son of God, who loved me, and gave himself for me"* (Galatians 2:20). Paul also exemplified this type of sacrifice in II Corinthians 1:8-9 as he said, *"For we would not, brethren, have you ignorant of our trouble which came to us in Asia, that we were pressed out of measure, above strength, insomuch that we despaired even of life: But we had the sentence of death in ourselves, that we should not trust in ourselves, but in God which raiseth the dead."*

Paul, through the pressure and persecutions of ministry, had lost all hope of life. But he continued living in God's strength and had faith in His providential plan. Paul did not wish that his fellow believers were ignorant of these burdens. He did not believe that they should be hidden behind cliches and anecdotes. But rather, later in the same letter, he specifies the very trials that he had endured as a minister of Christ. In II Corinthians 11:21-33 he writes, *"I speak as concerning reproach, as though we had been weak. Howbeit whereinsoever any is bold, (I speak foolishly,) I am bold also. Are they Hebrews? so am I. Are they Israelites? so am I. Are they the seed of Abraham? so am I. Are they ministers of Christ? (I speak as a fool) I am more; in labours more abundant, in stripes above measure, in prisons more frequent, in deaths oft. Of the Jews five times received I forty stripes save one. Thrice was I beaten with rods, once was I stoned, thrice I suffered shipwreck, a night and a day I have been in the deep; In journeyings often, in perils of waters, in perils of robbers, in perils by mine own countrymen, in perils by the heathen, in perils in the city, in perils in the wilderness, in perils in the sea, in perils among false brethren; In weariness and painfulness, in watchings often, in hunger and thirst, in fastings often, in cold and nakedness. Beside those things that* are *without, that which cometh upon me daily, the care of all the churches. . . . In Damascus the governor under Aretas the king kept the city of the Damascenes with a garrison, desirous to apprehend me: And through a window in a basket was I let down by the wall, and escaped his hands."* However, in the midst of Paul's honest presentation of his difficulties he never asked for pity, nor did he display a "victim" mentality. He declared boldly, *"Who is weak, and I am not weak? who is offended, and I burn not? If I must needs glory, I will glory of the things which concern mine infirmities. The God and Father of our Lord Jesus Christ, which is blessed for evermore, knoweth that I lie not"* (II Corinthians 11:29-31).

The secret to Paul's ability to be a *"living sacrifice"* is found in the first few verses of this letter where he presents his view of God and his ministry for God to fellow believers. II Corinthians 1:3-7 says, *"Blessed be God, even the Father of our Lord Jesus Christ, the Father of mercies, and the God of all comfort; Who comforteth us in all our tribulation, that we may be able to comfort them which are in any trouble, by the comfort wherewith we ourselves are comforted of God. For as the sufferings of Christ abound in us, so our consolation also aboundeth by Christ. And whether we be afflicted, it is for your consolation and salvation, which is effectual in the enduring of the same sufferings which we also suffer: or whether we be comforted, it is for your consolation and salvation. And our hope of you is stedfast, knowing, that as ye are partakers of the sufferings, so shall ye be also of the consolation."* Paul viewed God as his personal comforter for every one of life's and ministry's tribulations. He also viewed his sacrifice as service for others. He desired to provide consolation (comfort) and salvation to others, even at the cost of his own personal comfort.

Paul, while writing to the believers at Philippi says, *"According to my earnest expectation and my hope, that in nothing I shall be ashamed, but that with all boldness, as always, so now also Christ shall be magnified in my body, whether it be by life, or by death. For to me to live is Christ, and to die is gain. But if I live in the flesh, this is the fruit of my labour: yet what I shall choose I wot not. For I am in a strait betwixt two, having a desire to depart, and to be with Christ; which is far better: Nevertheless to abide in the flesh is more needful for you"* (Philippians 1:20-24). The sacrifices of this life are real for any servant of God. For the missionary, these sacrifices are magnified by the very nature of the work. He is called to prove his commitment to be Jesus's disciple not by His words but by His actions.

Jesus, while speaking to a multitude that was following Him, said in Luke 14:26-27, *"If any man come to me, and hate not his father, and mother, and wife, and children, and brethren, and sisters, yea, and his own life also, he cannot be my disciple. And whosoever doth not bear his cross, and come after me, cannot be my disciple."* And Matthew 10:37-39 clarifies Jesus's discipleship qualifications by saying, *"He that loveth father or mother more than me is not worthy of me: and he that loveth son or daughter more than me is not worthy of me. And he that taketh not his cross, and followeth after me, is not worthy of me. He that findeth his life shall lose it: and he that loseth his life for my sake shall find it."* He was sharing with those following Him on that day that the price of being His follower is the sacrifice of everything and everyone in their life for the love of Him. And because He did not desire the masses to unwittingly declare their commitment, He continues in Luke 14:28-33, *"For which of you, intending to build a tower, <u>sitteth not down first, and counteth the cost,</u> whether he have sufficient to finish it? Lest haply, after he hath laid the foundation, and is not able to finish it, all that behold it begin to mock him, Saying, This man began to build, and was not able to finish. Or what king, going to make war against another king, sitteth not down first, and consulteth whether he be able with ten thousand to meet him that cometh against him with twenty thousand? Or else, while the other is yet a great way off, he sendeth an ambassage, and desireth conditions of peace. <u>So likewise, whosoever he be of you that forsaketh not all that he hath, he cannot be my disciple."</u>*

Each believer must seriously count the cost of service. The next generation must be taught that, as good soldiers of the King of kings and Lord of lords, there is a price to be paid. The price is high, it is personal, it is financial, it is physical, and yet it is nothing in comparison to the price of *"the precious blood of Christ, as of a lamb without blemish and without spot,*" which He paid on Calvary for our soul (I Peter 1:18). Each believer must say with confident faith, "*For I reckon that the sufferings of this present time are not worthy to be compared with the glory which shall be revealed in us*" (Romans 8:18).

Please understand that the call to missionary work is not to be exalted nor glorified. Missionaries are simple servants. They are neither to be pitied nor pampered. However, the day to day challenges and changes that a missionary and his family face must be prepared for and prayed about by the missionary as well as fellow believers. There is no reason that missionaries and their personal testimonies and sacrifices should cause damage to the cause of Christ. On the contrary, if the subject of missions is handled with care by applying the truths of Scripture and a true faith in the all-wise and all-loving God, we will see the ministry of world-wide missions grow in strength and numbers in the generations to come.

My desire is that you may consider what role God has for you in the ministry of missions and dedicate yourself to be a faithful disciple of Jesus Christ as you are a "*living sacrifice*" to God (Romans 12:1).

I Thessalonians 3:1-8

1 Wherefore when we could no longer forbear,
we thought it good to be left at Athens alone;
2 And sent Timotheus, our brother, and minister of God,
and our fellowlabourer in the gospel of Christ,
to establish you, and to comfort you concerning your faith:
*3 **That no man should be moved by these afflictions:***
for yourselves know that we are appointed thereunto.
4 For verily, when we were with you,
we told you before that we should suffer tribulation;
even as it came to pass, and ye know.
5 For this cause, when I could no longer forbear,
I sent to know your faith,
lest by some means the tempter have tempted you,
and our labour be in vain.
6 But now when Timotheus came from you unto us,
and brought us good tidings of your faith and charity,
and that ye have good remembrance of us always,
desiring greatly to see us, as we also to see you:
*7 **Therefore, brethren,***
we were comforted over you in all our affliction
and distress by your faith:
*8 **For now we live, if ye stand fast in the Lord.***

Proverbs 22:3-4

*3 A prudent man foreseeth the evil, and hideth himself:
but the simple pass on, and are punished.
4 By humility and the fear of the LORD are
riches, and honour, and life.*

Introduction

MISSIONS:
THE JOYFUL HARVEST

Psalm 126:5-6
They that sow in tears shall reap in joy.
He that goeth forth and weepeth, bearing precious seed,
shall doubtless come again with rejoicing,
bringing his sheaves with him.

The ministry of missions provides many opportunities for rejoicing both on earth and in heaven. However, because many of God's laborers become *"weary in well doing,"* they often do not enjoy the *"season"* of joyful harvest (Galatians 6:9). One of the primary goals of this book is to help those who desire to participate in the ministry of missions to be accurately informed and adequately prepared for the labor they are entering.

In order for a farmer to enjoy his dream of a plentiful harvest, he must carefully prepare himself for the work that he must complete. Most importantly, he must choose the crop he wants to harvest. Then he must choose the proper seed, prepare his equipment, and prepare the soil by adding nutrition, irrigating, and plowing. When the time is right, he must carefully plant the chosen seed in the prepared soil. Finally, he must wait, wait, and wait some more as he carefully watches over and attends to the needs of his seeds by regular watering, weeding, etc. All the work that the farmer does to make sure that the little seed can produce the desired crop is hard and requires an extreme amount of patience, but when the harvest day comes and the plants are full of ripe fruit, the farmer experiences the joy of his investment. The farmer knows that this harvest was not produced overnight, nor did it develop on its own. The harvest required his investment through personal sacrifice and dedication, but it was worth it all.

The apostle Paul uses farming as a specific illustration for his ministry when he said *"I have planted, Apollos watered; but God gave the increase. . . . Now he that planteth and he that watereth are one: and every man shall receive his own reward according to his own labour"* (I Corinthians 3:6-8). Paul recognized that although he had planted the spiritual seed of God's Word in Corinth, time and sacrifice by himself and others were needed before that seed could produce its spiritual fruit through God's divine power. The ministry of missions is the same today, but sadly some missionaries never see the fruit of their sacrifice because they become discouraged and quit before the harvest is ready. Many of those who quit do so not because they did not have a true heart for God, nor because they did not have the correct goals in mind as they began, but because they simply did not realize the level of physical, emotional, and spiritual sacrifice that would be required and the length of time it would take before the harvest would be ready. For most missionaries, their first term is a time of preparing the soil and planting the seed. It is not until their second or third term that they truly enjoy the opportunity to *"come again with rejoicing, bringing his [their] sheaves with him [them]"* (Psalm 126:6).

The ministry of missions, whereby the *"precious seed"* of the Gospel of Jesus Christ is spread across the globe, is a great undertaking. When accomplished correctly and faithfully, it provides an overwhelming joy as the spiritual fruit is harvested for the glory of God (Psalm 126:5, Matthew 13:1-23). And every missionary can experience the same joys the Apostle Paul experienced—the joys of God's presence, God's promises, God's power, God's protection, God's purpose, and God's people.

The Joy of God's Presence

God's faithful minister can enjoy the constant presence of his Lord and Savior as he seeks to fulfill Jesus's command to *"Go ye therefore, and teach all nations, baptizing them in the name of the Father, and of the Son, and of the Holy Ghost: Teaching them to observe all things whatsoever I have commanded you*" (Matthew 28:19-20). Jesus concludes by promising, "*Lo, I am with you alway, even unto the end of the world. Amen*" (Matthew 28:20).

He can serve God in any situation or location with the knowledge that God has said, "*I will never leave thee, nor forsake thee. So that we may boldly say, The Lord is my helper, and I will not fear what man shall do unto me*" (Hebrews 13:5-6). As he finds himself in difficult situations, he can remember the Apostle Paul's experiences found in Acts 18:9-10, where God said to him, "*Be not afraid, but speak, and hold not thy peace: For I am with thee, and no man shall set on thee to hurt thee: for I have much people in this city.*" On those occasions when he has no human companions in the ministry, the missionary can say with the Apostle Paul, "*no man stood with me, but all men forsook me,*" and then conclude by saying, "*Notwithstanding the Lord stood with me, and strengthened me; that by me the preaching might be fully known, and that all the Gentiles might hear: and I was delivered out of the mouth of the lion. And the Lord shall deliver me from every evil work, and will preserve me unto his heavenly kingdom: to whom be glory for ever and ever. Amen*" (II Timothy 4:16-18).

The Joy of God's Promises

God's faithful minister can joyfully anticipate the fulfillment of God's promises of both earthly and heavenly rewards for his labor. He can expectantly trust God's promise that when His Word "*goeth forth . . . it shall not return unto me void, but it shall accomplish that which I please, and it shall prosper in the thing whereto I sent it. For ye shall go out with joy, and be led forth with peace*" (Isaiah 55:11-12). He can say with the Apostle Paul, "*For I reckon that the sufferings of this present time are not worthy to be compared with the glory which shall be revealed in us*" (Romans 8:18). And through the difficulties of ministry he can declare, "*But none of these things move me, neither count I my life dear unto myself, so that I might finish my course with joy, and the ministry, which I have received of the Lord Jesus, to testify the gospel of the grace of God*" (Acts 20:24). Then as he comes to the end of his life and ministry, he can say, "*I have fought a good fight, I have finished my course, I have kept the faith*" (II Timothy 4:7). He can confidently serve God knowing that in heaven "*there is laid up for me [him] a crown of righteousness, which the Lord, the righteous judge, shall give me [him] at that day: and not to me [him] only, but unto all them also that love his appearing*" (II Timothy 4:7-8).

The Joy of God's Power

God's faithful minister can enjoy the limitless power of his Almighty God in his life and ministry. Just as Jesus Christ promised, "*Ye shall receive power, after that the Holy Ghost is come upon you: and ye shall be witnesses unto me both in Jerusalem, and in all Judaea, and in Samaria, and unto the uttermost part of the earth*" (Acts 1:8). He can regularly depend on the Word of God, which "*is quick, and powerful, and sharper than any twoedged sword, piercing even to the dividing asunder of soul and spirit, and of the joints and marrow, and is a discerner of the thoughts and intents of the heart*" (Hebrews 4:12). He can confidently say with the Apostle Paul, "*For I am not ashamed of the gospel of Christ: for it is the power of God unto salvation to every one that believeth; to the Jew first, and also to the Greek*" (Romans 1:16). As he faithfully presents the Gospel of Christ to the lost around him, he can see the power of God "*to open their eyes, and to turn them from darkness to light, and from the power of Satan unto God, that they may receive forgiveness of sins, and inheritance among them which are sanctified by faith that is in me*" (Acts 26:18). Daily in his own personal life he can experience the "*exceeding greatness of his power to us-ward who believe, according to the working of his mighty power*" (Ephesians 1:19).

The Joy of God's Protection

God's faithful minister can face each event in his life with the joyful confidence of God's personal protection. He can go about his life and ministry with the same confidence that the Apostle Paul had when he said, "*But thou hast fully known my doctrine, manner of life, purpose, faith, longsuffering, charity, patience, persecutions, afflictions, which came unto me at Antioch, at Iconium, at Lystra; what persecutions I endured: but out of them all the Lord delivered me"* (II Timothy 3:10-11). He can face each danger in complete confidence that all the power of Satan and his angels will never touch him without God's specific and limited permission, because God has *"made an hedge about him"* (Job 1:8-12). By doing so he will obey Jesus's command to *"fear not them which kill the body, but are not able to kill the soul: but rather fear him which is able to destroy both soul and body in hell"* (Matthew 10:26-28).

The Joy of God's People

God's faithful minister has the joy of working with and ministering to God's children, who are also his spiritual brothers and sisters. He has the opportunity to rejoice as their lives are changed and matured to be more like Christ through his ministry (II Corinthians 2:3, 7:4, 13). He also has the opportunity to encourage them to stay faithful to God as he shares with them the joy they are producing in his life, just as the Apostle Paul indicated to the believers in Philippi, *"Therefore, my brethren dearly beloved and longed for, my joy and crown, so stand fast in the Lord, my dearly beloved"* (Philippians 4:1). He can say, as the Apostle Paul did to the believers in Thessalonica, *"For ye are our glory and joy"* (I Thessalonians 1:20). He will anticipate the future joy of continued ministry with them and to them by saying, *"For what thanks can we render to God again for you, for all the joy wherewith we joy for your sakes before our God"* (I Thessalonians 3:9, III John 1:4).

The Joy of God's Purpose

God's faithful minister can experience the joy of knowing that he is fulfilling his created purpose. I Corinthians 5:17 says, *"Therefore if any man be in Christ, he is a new creature: old things are passed away; behold, all things are become new."* And verse 20 provides the purpose for each new creature's life by adding, *"now then we are ambassadors for Christ."* A faithful minister of God has the opportunity to have the most purposeful life possible as he continues the work for the Lord Jesus Christ by being *"the light of the world,"* by distributing the light of the Gospel to those who live in darkness (Matthew 5:14). As he patiently serves God through trials and temptations, he has the blessed privilege of saying with the Apostle Paul, *"But none of these things move me, neither count I my life dear unto myself, so that I might finish my course with joy, and the ministry, which I have received of the Lord Jesus, to testify the gospel of the grace of God"* (Acts 20:24).

Now that we have explored some of the joys of a faithful missionary's life, let us follow Jesus's example of self-sacrificial faithfulness as we minister, by always *"looking unto Jesus the author and finisher of our faith; who for the joy that was set before him endured the cross, despising the shame, and is set down at the right hand of the throne of God"* (Hebrews 12:1). Let us remember that *"no man, having put his hand to the plough, and looking back, is fit for the kingdom of God"* (Luke 9:62). Let us be wise to count *"the cost"* of the ministry so that we may be properly prepared for the personal sacrifice that will be required and remember that it is an investment that produces the future joy of a God-blessed harvest (Luke 14:25-33).

II Corinthians 4:1-5

*1 **Therefore seeing we have this ministry,***
as we have received mercy, we faint not;
2 But have renounced the hidden things of dishonesty,
not walking in craftiness,
nor handling the word of God deceitfully;
but by manifestation of the truth commending ourselves
to every man's conscience in the sight of God.
*3 **But if our gospel be hid, it is hid to them that are lost:***
4 In whom the god of this world hath blinded the minds
of them which believe not,
lest the light of the glorious gospel of Christ,
who is the image of God, should shine unto them.
*5 **For we preach not ourselves, but Christ Jesus the Lord;***
and ourselves your servants for Jesus' sake.
*16 **For which cause we faint not;***
but though our outward man perish,
yet the inward man is renewed day by day.
17 For our light affliction, which is but for a moment,
worketh for us a far more exceeding and eternal weight of glory;
18 While we look not at the things which are seen,
but at the things which are not seen:
for the things which are seen are temporal;
but the things which are not seen are eternal.

The Missionary's Comfort and Counsel
As He Adjusts
To His New Life and Ministry

A realistic view
of the missionary experience
and the Biblical truths needed
to stay faithful in the ministry

Chapter 1

ARE YOU SURE?

Acts 21:12-14
And when we heard these things,
both we, and they of that place,
besought him not to go up to Jerusalem.
Then Paul answered,
What mean ye to weep and to break mine heart?
for I am ready not to be bound only,
but also to die at Jerusalem for the name of the Lord Jesus.
And when he would not be persuaded, we ceased, saying,
The will of the Lord be done.

The Missionary's Experience

The spiritual battle against a missionary preparing for service starts long before he ever lands on foreign soil. From the very moment that he recognizes God's call upon his life, he is faced with constant attacks from Satan with the direct purpose of distracting or discouraging him from being a faithful steward *"of the mysteries of God"* (I Corinthians 4:1).

One of the most effective and devastating attacks from Satan against the missionary is often found in the "loving" words and counsel of others. It is not uncommon for a preparing missionary to share his passion and dedication to leave all for the cause of Christ, only to receive doubt-filled responses like: "Are you sure?" or "Well, I'm behind you if you really think that is what God wants" or "Wow, that is a big sacrifice!" What is even more devastating are the comments made behind his back, such as: "I think someone should talk to him about that" or "I'm not sure he's cut out for that type of life" or "Does he know what he is getting himself into?" These devastating detractors from the will of God have eliminated many missionaries from ever getting to the field. They have also been part of Satan's arsenal of fiery darts of doubt to destroy many missionaries after they arrive on their field of service and begin to face difficult times. Perhaps the missionary's greatest burden is not the comments themselves but rather that they are being shared by the very people who should "know" and "love" him most. The preparing missionary may even come to realize that these human concerns are logically legitimate and that, although these reactions are contrary to his plans, they are being shared in "human love" for him. Therefore, he comes to the great crossroads of choosing human reasoning or divine enablement.

Biblical Examples

Dear servant of God, the Apostle Paul faced similar concerns and comments from fellow believers and friends as they *"besought him not to go up to Jerusalem"* (Acts 21:12). In Acts 21:8-11, Agabus prophesies about the result of Paul's determination to minister in Jerusalem. Therefore, with great love for Paul, his fellow travel companions, as well as the believers in Caesarea, began to plead with him to not fulfill his ministry plans (Acts 21:12). The loving evaluations and concerns of fellow believers for Paul were legitimate, but Paul would not be distracted or discouraged from obeying God's calling. Paul's response: *"What mean ye to weep and to break mine heart?"* displays that Paul did not ignore the loving concerns of others, nor was he in denial of the realities he was facing (Acts 21:13). His heart was breaking because of their sorrow, but he still declared, *"I am ready not to be bound only, but also to die at Jerusalem for the name of the Lord Jesus"* (Acts 21:13). But Satan knows the devastating effect of the tears and words of others. He knows that our heart and spirit can be broken quickly through human counsel that does not take into account either the will or greatness of

God. Moses and the children of Israel are a clear example of such discouragement when they received reports about the Promised Land from the twelve spies. God had promised them great blessings, and the children of Israel had physical evidence of great rewards provided by the spies as *"they came unto the brook of Eshcol, and cut down from thence a branch with one cluster of grapes, and they bare it between two upon a staff; and they brought of the pomegranates, and of the figs"* (Numbers 13:23). Even the initial accounting of their investigation verified what God had promised as they said, *"We came unto the land whither thou sentest us, and surely it floweth with milk and honey; and this is the fruit of it"* (Numbers 13:27). But the limited view of man's logic quickly destroyed the greatness of God's provision, as the ten spies continued, *"Nevertheless the people be strong that dwell in the land, and the cities are walled, and very great: and moreover we saw the children of Anak there. The Amalekites dwell in the land of the south: and the Hittites, and the Jebusites, and the Amorites, dwell in the mountains: and the Canaanites dwell by the sea, and by the coast of Jordan"* (Numbers 13:28-29). Although *"Caleb stilled the people before Moses, and said, Let us go up at once, and possess it; for we are well able to overcome it,"* he could not regain the confidence that the doubt-filled reports had destroyed (Numbers 13:30).

And as the ten spies continued to share their *"evil report,"* they said, *"We be not able to go up against the people; for they are stronger than we. . . . The land, through which we have gone to search it, is a land that eateth up the inhabitants thereof; and all the people that we saw in it are men of a great stature. And there we saw the giants, the sons of Anak, which come of the giants: and we were in our own sight as grasshoppers, and so we were in their sight"* (Numbers 13:31-33). Following such counsel, *"all the congregation lifted up their voice, and cried; and the people wept that night. And all the children of Israel murmured against Moses and against Aaron: and the whole congregation said unto them, Would God that we had died in the land of Egypt! or would God we had died in this wilderness! And wherefore hath the LORD brought us unto this land, to fall by the sword, that our wives and our children should be a prey? were it not better for us to return into Egypt? And they said one to another, Let us make a captain, and let us return into Egypt"* (Numbers 14:1-3). The heart and spirit of the children of Israel were devastated, and they wanted to return to the place from which they had come—a place of slavery and torture, but at least a place in which they did not need to trust in God. They had all the promises of God's blessing if they would only obey in faith, but due to a few discouraging comments, they were ready to quit. Thankfully, Paul nor his companions maintained the same spirit. Paul declared his dedication to obey God at any cost, and with tears in their eyes but strength in their heart they *"ceased"* trying to prevent Paul from his ministry and said, *"The will of the Lord be done"* (Acts 21:14).

Actual Events

Each prospective missionary faces doubtful comments to different degrees and for different reasons. I am very thankful for my Christian family and for their focus on full-time Christian ministry. I am also very grateful for a supportive sending pastor and church. But these privileges did not eliminate the funny looks and doubtful comments. Some comments were made by extended family who simply did not understand and did not want to see us leave, while others came from fellow believers who simply looked at some of the outward appearances and situations.

I can recall one common subject of doubt in reference to my age (not my actual age but my appearance of age). I had even been advised to wait a few more years before stepping into missions, not to gain more experience in ministry, but simply so that I would appear older and more mature. And as I considered these concerns that God permitted me to hear, I found comfort in God's personal knowledge of me, my age, and my ministry calling through the example of Jeremiah. *"Then said I, Ah, Lord GOD! behold, I cannot speak: for I am a child. But the LORD said unto me, Say not, I am a child: for thou shalt go to all that I shall send thee, and whatsoever I command thee thou shalt speak. Be not afraid of their faces: for I am with thee to deliver thee, saith the LORD. Then the LORD put forth his hand, and touched my mouth. And the LORD said unto me, Behold, I have put my words in thy mouth. See, I have this day set thee over the nations and over the kingdoms, to root out, and to pull down, and to destroy, and to throw down, to build, and to plant*" (Jeremiah 1:6-10). I also recall comments and concerned looks about our needed budget in order to fulfill our ministry purpose. And yet God provided guiding comfort through His command to "*seek ye the kingdom of God*" with his promise that "*all these things shall be added unto you*" (Matthew 6:33).

Biblical Exhortation

Dear servant of God, you must never permit Satan to discourage you through the doubt-filled comments of others. You must constantly guard yourself from destructive human reasoning, which discounts God's will and power in your life and ministry. At the same time, you must ask God to provide you with wise counsel, which will provide a realistic understanding of yourself and your plans as you step out by faith (Proverbs 24:6). As God permits you to receive both counsel and criticism, you must say with David, "*Is there not a cause?*" as you set your heart and actions upon obedience no matter the outcome (I Samuel 17:29).

Practical Participation

🖎 **Missionary Candidate - Please prepare** for those doubt-filled darts of Satan that will come at you as you seek to obey God. Please know that many of these doubts are simply well-meaning expressions of concern from those who love you and believe they are seeking what is best for your life and safety. Do not become discouraged, but rather turn to God more earnestly to truly know His will and strength through the knowledge of and obedience to His Word.

🖎 **Missionary's Supporter - Please pray** for the prospective missionary as he interacts with those who may discourage him from fulfilling God's will for his life. Pray that he will constantly be reminded of God's presence and power to fulfill each and every part of God's will for his life, no matter the price. **Please provide** him with encouraging words of Scripture and godly counsel as he seeks to evaluate the criticisms and concerns he receives. Provide him with constant assurance of your support as he seeks to obey God, no matter the consequences.

🖎 **Missionary in Service - Please press on.** Do not allow the present or past doubts of others distract you from the perfect will of God for your life. Look to God for His counsel and trust Him to be the supplier of every need. Be assured that no matter what you may face, you are always safest and most blessed as you stay in the center of God's will.

Increase Your Faith

Jeremiah 32:27
27 Behold, I am the LORD, the God of all flesh:
is there any thing too hard for me?

Philippians 4:12-13
12 I know both how to be abased,
and I know how to abound:
every where and in all things I am instructed
both to be full and to be hungry,
both to abound and to suffer need.
13 I can do all things through Christ
which strengtheneth me.

Romans 8:37
37 Nay, in all these things we are more than conquerors
through him that loved us.

Mark 10:27
27 And Jesus looking upon them saith,
With men it is impossible, but not with God:
for with God all things are possible.

II Corinthians 4:7
7 But we have this treasure in earthen vessels,
that the excellency of the power may be of God,
and not of us.

Romans 10:17
So then faith cometh by hearing,
and hearing by the word of God.

Examples of Like Faith

David
I Samuel 17:22-58

Nehemiah
Nehemiah 4:1-23

Jesus
John 7:1-10, Mark 3:21

Romans 15:4
For whatsoever things were written aforetime
were written for our learning,
that we through patience and comfort of the scriptures
might have hope.

Chapter 2

UNTIL WE MEET AGAIN

Acts 20:36-37
And when he had thus spoken,
he kneeled down, and prayed with them all.
And they all wept sore, and fell on Paul's neck, and kissed him,
Sorrowing most of all for the words which he spake,
that they should see his face no more.
And they accompanied him unto the ship.

The Missionary's Experience

The final days and hours in the missionary's homeland are filled with a mixture of anticipation and trepidation. For months and even years he has talked of this great adventure on which he is about to embark. He has stood in front of crowds and proclaimed his dedication and determination, and now the time has come for him to leave the very ones who shared his dreams. His spiritual passion drives him forward, but the private moments, those last days and hours with family and friends, are filled with sorrow and tears. He can now proclaim with the Apostle Paul, "*I am ready not to be bound only, but also to die at Jerusalem for the name of the Lord Jesus,*" as he takes his first steps toward such an end (Acts 21:13). He is loading his belongings on a ship and placing himself (and his family) on a plane with the very real possibility that this "good-bye" will be his last on this earth. And so he has determined that God's call is more important to him than any earthly relationship, and he rehearses in his mind the words of his Lord, "*If any man come to me, and hate not his father, and mother, and wife, and children, and brethren, and sisters, yea, and his own life also, he cannot be my disciple. And whosoever doth not bear his cross, and come after me, cannot be my disciple*" (Luke 14:26-27). Then he finds himself weeping, falling on the necks of those dear to him, kissing them good-bye, and saying, "Until we meet again" (Acts 20:36).

Biblical Examples

Dear servant of God, there are some today who may not understand the extreme pain you may face in the final weeks and days before your departure to your field of service. Some would even think poorly of you if you were to publicly display your grieving because you are a "Missionary," and for some reason missionaries are seen as being different from other believers. It is as if they are to rejoice in our departure, looking only at the spiritual opportunities, without facing the human realities of personal loss. However, those who think of us in this way fail to understand "*we also are men of like passions*" (Acts 14:15). While we are touched by the very joys and sorrows they experience, they have not been called upon to make the same sacrifice and, therefore, are not overwhelmed with the same sorrow.

You are not alone in your sorrow nor in your sacrifice. Throughout the history of missions, others have stood on the docks (as Paul's friends did) or at the departure terminal of airports, and when no words could describe their thoughts, their actions declared their heart. Their tears displayed their love for family and friends as their steps forward to board the craft declared their love for their God. You must guard yourself from being like those who, when Jesus said, "*Follow me*," replied with "*Lord, suffer me first to go and bury my father.*" Jesus's command for our life is clear: "*Let the dead bury their dead: but go thou and preach the kingdom of God*" (Luke 9:59-60). You must also not delay your departure as the one who said to Jesus, "*Lord, I will follow thee; but let me first go bid them farewell, which are at home at my house. And Jesus said unto him, No man, having put his hand to the plough, and looking back, is fit for the kingdom of God*" (Luke 9:61-62).

It is not wrong for you to sorrow, but it is wrong for you to "turn back." Accept these emotions as part of God's plan for your life. Know that they are not meant to destroy you but to provide you with the privileged opportunity to lay at God's feet your sacrifice as a symbol of your love for Him. I encourage you to remember your own courageous words about the worthiness of the cause spoken in public and to live them in private. Follow Paul's example as he declared, *"But I keep under my body, and bring it into subjection: lest that by any means, when I have preached to others, I myself should be a castaway"* (I Corinthians 9:27). Set your sights on the promises of God and don't look back. Remember that *"Jesus answered and said, Verily I say unto you, There is no man that hath left house, or brethren, or sisters, or father, or mother, or wife, or children, or lands, for my sake, and the gospel's, but he shall receive an hundredfold now in this time, houses, and brethren, and sisters, and mothers, and children, and lands, with persecutions; and in the world to come eternal life. But many that are first shall be last; and the last first"* (Matthew 19:28-30). Sorrow, hug, kiss, and then do not say "Good-bye," but rather, "Until we meet again," whether on this earth or in heaven.

Actual Events

I can remember the final months before leaving for my field of service as being some of the darkest days of my spiritual life; days in which many never knew the pain I was feeling. I can recall specifically leaving my parents' home for the last time, just a few weeks before our departure, and thinking to myself as I drove away, "This is it, I will not see them again on this side of heaven." Some would call that being overly dramatic. But is it? We are taught as missionaries that we must "burn our bridges." We are to "end our lives here at home and start anew," looking for the *"hundredfold"* promised to all those who leave *"house, or brethren, or sisters, or father, or mother, or wife, or children, or lands, for my sake, and the gospel's."* God's promises are true. Therefore, *"let us hold fast the profession of our faith without wavering; (for he is faithful that promised)"* (Hebrews 10:23). But while we put our faith to action, we must not deny or cover up the emotions and spiritual battles we face. For me, I looked upon each of those moments as a spiritual funeral in which I was either *permitting* my precious human relationships to be put to death for Christ or I was *rejecting* Christ's death to purchase ownership of my life. I had no choice but to choose Christ over family and friends. As I packed our belongings, visited family and friends, and had our last service in our home church, the sorrow was at times overwhelming; yet the need to obey was infinitely greater. I was raised on the idea that "obedience is the very best way to show that you believe." Now I needed to make the choice to sacrifice my world to prove my belief in the King of kings and Lord of lords. These steps of obedience were not made publicly, but privately. They were made in the face of direct rebellion by everything called *"me."* It was not *"my"* nature to reject family. It was not *"my"* desire to set out on an unknown adventure. It was not *"my"* strength which packed boxes and luggage to be shipped. Everything I was physically doing was contrary to *"my"* flesh. But, as I sought daily for God's strength, He permitted me *"to be strengthened with might by his Spirit in the inner man,"* to keep me on the path of obedience (Ephesians 3:16).

Biblical Exhortation

Dear servant of God, it is of the utmost importance that you recognize that this is your choice. You have the choice to allow the Holy Spirit to strengthen you or you can be overcome with sorrow and fear. Neither your mother, father, friend, or pastor can make you obey nor can they go with you as you depart. You must choose to follow Abram's example of obedience by packing and departing, knowing that you are guaranteed God's blessing and presence (Genesis 12:1-6, Matthew 28:19-20).

Practical Participation

✍ **Missionary Candidate - Please prepare** for the sorrow of departure by knowing that it is different for each missionary. Know that no matter what those final days bring to you, you must be obedient. God's call is always worth the sacrifice. And He is always faithful in His promises. You must take the time now to make God and His Word the most important things in your life. You must dedicate your life to obedience at all earthly cost.

✍ **Missionary's Supporter - Please pray** for the missionary's final days before he leaves all he considers dear. Not just for the details of shipping or travel safety, but for the spiritual strength to follow through with his calling for the glory of his King. **Please provide** opportunities for him to weep when it is needed, and then give him the assurance of your faithful prayers as you send him on his way.

✍ **Missionary in Service - Please press on.** Know that you are not alone. It is true that by following through with your missionary calling you are joining a select group of believers. Those who have gone on before you have both testified and proven with their actions that God's promises will never fail you. Allow your physical eyes to be filled with tears while you turn your spiritual eyes to your Savior.

Increase Your Faith

Matthew 16:24-27

24 Then said Jesus unto his disciples,
If any man will come after me, let him deny himself,
and take up his cross, and follow me.
25 For whosoever will save his life shall lose it:
and whosoever will lose his life for my sake shall find it.
26 For what is a man profited,
if he shall gain the whole world,
and lose his own soul?
or what shall a man give in exchange for his soul?
27 For the Son of man shall come
in the glory of his Father
with his angels;
and then he shall reward every man
according to his works.

Luke 9:59-62

59 And he said unto another, Follow me.
But he said, Lord, suffer me first to go and bury my father.
60 Jesus said unto him, Let the dead bury their dead:
but go thou and preach the kingdom of God.
61 And another also said, Lord, I will follow thee;
but let me first go bid them farewell,
which are at home at my house.
62 And Jesus said unto him,
No man, having put his hand to the plough,
and looking back,
is fit for the kingdom of God.

Ephesians 3:16

16 That he would grant you,
according to the riches of his glory,
to be strengthened with might by his Spirit
in the inner man;

I Corinthians 9:27

27 But I keep under my body, and bring it into subjection:
lest that by any means, when I have preached to others,
I myself should be a castaway.

Hebrews 10:23

23 Let us hold fast the profession of our faith
without wavering;
(for he is faithful that promised;)

Matthew 19:29-30

29 And every one that hath forsaken houses,
or brethren, or sisters,
or father, or mother, or wife, or children, or lands,
for my name's sake,
shall receive an hundredfold,
and shall inherit everlasting life.
30 But many that are first shall be last
and the last shall be first.

Romans 10:17

So then faith cometh by hearing,
and hearing by the word of God.

Examples of Like Faith

Noah
Genesis 6:8-7:16

Abram
Genesis 12:1-6
Hebrews 11:8-10

Abraham's Servant and Rebecca
Genesis 24:51-61

Paul
Acts 20:17-38, 21:3-15

Romans 15:4
For whatsoever things were written aforetime
were written for our learning,
that we through patience and comfort of the scriptures
might have hope.

Chapter 3

IMMINENT DECISIONS

Hebrews 11:8-9
By faith Abraham,
when he was called to go out into a place
which he should after receive for an inheritance, obeyed;
and he went out, not knowing whither he went.
By faith he sojourned in the land of promise,
as in a strange country,
dwelling in tabernacles with Isaac and Jacob,
the heirs with him of the same promise:

The Missionary's Experience

As the missionary departs his homeland, he faces many challenges: planning, packing, and then the "fair wells." None of these things compare to the confusion of landing in a foreign country, where his ability to communicate has been eliminated. Add to that the obvious cultural differences (clothing, food, music, etc.), and it becomes obvious that he is an alien (pilgrim, foreigner) in a new world. With the speed of modern-day travel, this confusion is intensified because he wakes up in one culture, climate, and language, and goes to sleep the same day in another. As a world traveler, he experiences immeasurable change to his entire world within a matter of a few hours. To add to the pressures, he may be forced through large lines where he is expected to answer numerous questions (presented in a foreign language or in broken English), which seem intrusive and to which he may not have all the answers (i.e., Where is your identification? Do you have any family or friends here? Where are you staying? What form of transportation will you be using? How long will you be visiting? etc.). Then he faces the baggage claim, or as it should be called, the "lost and confiscated." There he may find that most of his private possessions have been rummaged through and perhaps are now even missing.

After gathering up what is left of his belongings and paying any import taxes demanded, he must then exit the "security" of an international airport (where there is some diplomatic interaction) to enter the "real" world, a world in which the signs mean nothing, the sounds coming out of the natives mouths remind him of the tower of Babel, and the smells and sights seem to come from another planet, not to mention the crowd of peddlers and beggars who surround him as he takes his first steps outside the airport doors. The thought then hits him like a brick, "What have I gotten myself into, and what am I doing here?"

Were it not for the friendly smile from the one calling his name (in an unusual accent) to gain his attention, and the help in loading his belongings into a vehicle and driving him to his temporary residence, he would purchase a ticket on the next available flight back to "NORMAL." Then the dreadful greeting comes, "Welcome to your new home. What do you think? Do you like it?" How does the missionary answer? He isn't even sure where he is, let alone what is going on around him. But with all of this confusion, he will need to make some of the greatest decisions of his life, and those decisions are imminent. Within the first hours and days, he will need to find reliable transportation, suitable housing, furnishings, food, etc. Then he will need to begin the process of finding the proper location for his new ministry. Somehow, while his head is spinning, he has to find the correct location to plant his feet to start his new life. Added to all of these pressures, his task becomes even more daunting as he encounters nationals who would not hesitate to make personal gain out of his confusion. The missionary begins to feel as though he is walking in the dark, but the darkness he is experiencing is not that of a safe home with only a few toys left on the floor. It is the darkness of a mountain cave with jagged edges and poisonous insects that could bring long-term damage.

Biblical Examples

Dear servant of God, these events are not exaggerated nor embellished. The first few minutes, hours, and days in your new homeland can be some of the most exciting and, at the same time, some of the most dreadful of your entire life. They are full of new things, things which, if you could understand what they were, you might enjoy. However, because your are not a tourist with a tour guide explaining each new encounter, you are left to the mercy of kind nationals or to fend for yourself. These are the same realities that many businessmen have faced as they travel around the world. One of my family members shared with me his experience of landing in a foreign country for the first time. His story matches the description just presented. But his stay was temporary–yours is permanent! Those things he found to be strange and even irritating did not need to become the "new norm."

Abraham faced similar experiences. He was not only called upon to leave his homeland by faith, he was called to be a "***stranger***" in a new land (Genesis 17:8). And when his wife Sarah died, he humbly asked the sons of Seth, the people of Canaan, to help him find a burial place for her by saying, "***I am a stranger and a sojourner with you: give me a possession of a burying place with you, that I may bury my dead out of my sight***" (Genesis 23:4). The burden of being a foreigner in a new land was not just borne by Abraham, but his son Isaac continued to "***sojourn in this land***" (Genesis 26:3); and in return he received the same promise that God gave to his father: "***Sojourn in this land, and I will be with thee, and will bless thee; for unto thee, and unto thy seed, I will give all these countries, and I will perform the oath which I sware unto Abraham thy father***" (Genesis 26:3). "***By faith he [Abraham] sojourned in the land of promise, as in a strange country***" (Hebrews 11:9). He left behind all he knew in order to dwell in an unknown land with new foods, languages, cultures, and climates. He did not bear this burden alone, but his wife and children bore it with him. And by doing so, they also experienced the promised presence of God throughout their lives. Although they needed to rely upon the strangers around them, God always provided his protection and provision when they trusted Him.

Sadly, the children of Abraham did not always trust God when they entered new lands. In Joshua 9:1-16 we find that the men of Gibeon *"did work wilily"* and lied about their identity and purpose as they pursued a pact with Joshua and Israel. Sadly, *"the men took of their victuals, and asked not counsel at the mouth of the LORD. And Joshua made peace with them, and made a league with them, to let them live: and the princes of the congregation sware unto them."* The Gibeonites became a burden to the children of Israel for years to come. Be sure to ask God for His wisdom and protection for each new encounter and decision you face, and then by faith, step forward, knowing that He *"giveth to all men liberally, and upbraideth not"* (James 1:5-8).

Actual Events

My experience of arriving in my new homeland was very different from that of most missionaries. I had the privilege of visiting my field of service five times before landing that final time as a missionary. Each time I arrived at the same airport and proceeded through the same steps. But on that final arrival, my view was different. Before, I was visiting. Now I was staying. The signs in the new language that I had ignored before now screamed at me, as if to say, "You will never understand me! Don't even try!" Now I felt the pressure of making major decisions, not just for myself, but for my wife and children. I was not just a tourist who would laugh at my foolish mistakes after returning home. I was a permanent resident and would suffer the consequences of my mistakes for years to come.

Within the first hours after arriving in my field of service, I was confronted with making the most expensive purchase of my life to date—a new vehicle. Although we had prayed for such a purchase, now I was signing on the dotted line, and I was not even sure the exact details of what I was signing. Humanly, I was at the mercy of a used car salesman in a foreign country. Spiritually, I signed the documents with only one security—faith that God was at work. Do not think of me as a man of faith for this choice. I assure you that God's provision came through the prayers of many, and I did not sign for the car until I was strongly encouraged to do so by my father-in-law, who God provided to nudge me down the path of faith.

Just a few months later, a kind and concerned neighbor warned me to never make any purchases or make any agreements without having a national friend with me. He stated very clearly that his own countrymen would seek to take advantage of me as a newcomer. Sadly, after being in the country for several years, another kind neighbor gave me almost the same warning. For this reason, I frequently find myself in the difficult and confusing situation of making important decisions with little or no information. And the information that I may find is often provided by people who, like *"one of themselves, even a prophet of their own, said, The Cretians [nationals] are alway liars, evil beasts, slow bellies"* (Titus 1:12). I have determined that the process of sojourning in a foreign land can be a great adventure. However, each adventure is not simply a new experience but rather an opportunity for me to see God fulfill His promise to guide me in accordance to His will, to the right people and places, in spite of my human ignorance.

Biblical Exhortation

Dear servant of God, you must not be overwhelmed by your physical surroundings or be destroyed by your lack of understanding. This is all God's plan for your life. As you take your first step away from the airport (the normal) and into the unknown, make a spiritual choice to move forward in faith. Remember that *"The steps of a good man are ordered by the LORD: and he delighteth in his way"* (Psalm 37:23). Each choice you make while being a *"good man"* (obedient to God's will) will not be a step in the dark or unknown but rather a walk with your "Daddy" on a path that He has already walked and specifically prepared for you (Romans 8:5). These moments are some of the best you will ever have to prove your dedication to *"trust in the LORD with all thine heart; and lean not unto thine own understanding. In all thy ways acknowledge him, and* [experience the fulfillment of God's promise that] *he shall direct thy paths*" (Proverbs 3:5-6).

Practical Participation

🖋 **Missionary Candidate - Please prepare** for the great adventures that lie ahead by viewing them as God's perfectly planned path on which He desires to guide you. Becoming a missionary means permanent changes to all that you have called "normal." The process may be shocking, so begin now to prepare yourself by viewing the minor present-day adjustments to your plans and daily life as God's training ground for your future ministry. Begin now to make a list of verses to remind you of God's plans for and presence in your life. Memorize those verses and document them, placing them in strategic places (wallet, purse, car), which will bring them continually to your attention while making them easily accessible in any time of need.

🖋 **Missionary's Supporter - Please pray** for the missionary to have calmness of spirit and clarity of mind as he steps into a totally new world and experiences almost complete helplessness while making major decisions. Pray that God will provide honest and helpful people on a daily basis so that he might be able to make right choices and find comfort in chaos. **Please provide** a listening ear and wise counsel when your missionary is attempting to make difficult decisions for his new life and ministry.

🖋 **Missionary in Service - Please press on** by trusting God to place each of your steps of faith in accordance to His perfectly prepared plan for your life and ministry. Do not allow the strangeness of the people and places you experience to turn you away from the normality of your personal walk with God. Rather, allow these experiences to help you cherish what can never be taken away from you: a personal Heavenly Father, who will always understand you, and His Word, which will never fail you.

Increase Your Faith

Psalm 37:1, 3-4, 23-24

1 Fret not thyself because of evildoers,
neither be thou envious against the workers of iniquity.
3 Trust in the LORD, and do good;
so shalt thou dwell in the land, and verily thou shalt be fed.
4 Delight thyself also in the LORD;
and he shall give thee the desires of thine heart.
23 The steps of a good man are ordered by the LORD:
and he delighteth in his way.
24 Though he fall, he shall not be utterly cast down:
for the LORD upholdeth him with his hand.

Proverbs 3:5-6

5 Trust in the LORD with all thine heart;
and lean not unto thine own understanding.
6 In all thy ways acknowledge him,
and he shall direct thy paths.

Matthew 6:9-13

9 After this manner therefore pray ye:
Our Father which art in heaven, Hallowed be thy name.
10 Thy kingdom come.
Thy will be done in earth, as it is in heaven.
11 Give us this day our daily bread.
12 And forgive us our debts, as we forgive our debtors.
13 And lead us not into temptation,
but deliver us from evil:
For thine is the kingdom, and the power, and the glory,
for ever. Amen.

Matthew 28:18-20

18 And Jesus came and spake unto them, saying,
All power is given unto me in heaven and in earth.
19 Go ye therefore, and teach all nations,
baptizing them in the name of the Father,
and of the Son, and of the Holy Ghost:
20 Teaching them to observe all things
whatsoever I have commanded you:
and, lo, I am with you alway,
even unto the end of the world.
Amen.

Luke 12:29-31

29 And seek not ye what ye shall eat, or what ye shall drink,
neither be ye of doubtful mind.
30 For all these things do the nations of the world seek after:
and your Father knoweth that ye have need of these things.
31 But rather seek ye the kingdom of God;
and all these things shall be added unto you.

Hebrews 13:5

5 Let your conversation be without covetousness;
and be content with such things as ye have:
for he hath said, I will never leave thee, nor forsake thee.

Romans 10:17
So then faith cometh by hearing,
and hearing by the word of God.

Examples of Like Faith

Abram
Genesis 12:1-20
(negative example)

Daniel, Shadrach, Meshach, and Abednego
Daniel 1:1-21

Romans 15:4
For whatsoever things were written aforetime
were written for our learning,
that we through patience and comfort of the scriptures
might have hope.

Chapter 4

PICTIONARY & CHARADES

I Corinthians 14:9-11
So likewise ye,
except ye utter by the tongue words easy to be understood,
how shall it be known what is spoken?
for ye shall speak into the air.
There are, it may be, so many kinds of voices in the world,
and none of them is without signification.
Therefore if I know not the meaning of the voice,
I shall be unto him that speaketh a barbarian,
and he that speaketh shall be a barbarian unto me.

The Missionary's Experience

The missionary is accustomed to being a communicator. He has had the privilege of standing before both small and large crowds for the purpose of communicating his plans and passion. But, as he arrives on his field of service, he makes one very obvious yet dreadful discovery: he can't communicate at all. Within the first hours and days, he encounters the very same need for himself and his family that he had faced many times as he traveled from town to town and church to church: the need to purchase food and daily living supplies. However, now he realizes that he does not understand the street signs to direct him to the nearest stores, and when he does arrive at a "store" (of sorts), all of the labels are in a language that he has yet to master. His confusion and frustration continues to grow as he tries to ask for help and finds that he has no way to communicate his needs. Time after time he repeats calmly but disappointedly, "No! No! I didn't mean that," all the while relying on the skills he learned while playing Pictionary and Charades. Throughout the next few weeks and months, God graciously permits him to assemble a few words and sentences, and some of the initial disappointment subsides. But as he remembers that his purpose for living in this new country is not just survival, but to share the Gospel with the nationals, his heart once again sinks. He understands that ministry demands communication, communication that is clear and that teaches each person in the language of his heart. Yet he discovers that even as he opens a native hymnal, the familiarity of the tunes is drowned out by the confusion of the words. So, he asks himself, "If I struggle to ask for milk and eggs, how am I ever going to share the Water of Life?" (John 4:14, Revelation 21:6). And when he desperately asks a veteran missionary (of forty years) about the length of time he struggled with the language, he is honestly but graciously informed that even after living more of his life in this foreign country than in his own homeland, he is still making mistakes and learning new things on a daily basis. The new missionary begins to realize that his battle of clearly communicating his thoughts and the Word of God will be fought for the rest of his life. So, as God opens opportunities to listen to those who need counsel, he will find his prayer to be threefold: "Oh, Lord please help me to understand clearly the words spoken; help me to have the clarity of mind to find your answers in a native Bible; and, finally, please provide me with the correct words and correct sounds from my mouth as I seek to impart Your wisdom to heal this broken heart." And as he enters the pulpit, he prays, "Oh, Lord please protect my unclear, poorly articulated, and improperly conjugated words from causing distractions from, and even damage to, your Word." And on a daily basis, while attempting to accomplish the simplest of tasks, he prays, "Oh, Lord please allow me the clarity of thought to both communicate my needs clearly, as well as understand the instruction I need to accomplish the tasks at hand. Help me to discern correctly the signs and labels around me, so that I do not lose my way or make incorrect and wasteful purchases."

Biblical Examples

Dear servant of God, communication is essential for your life and ministry in your new home. The confusion you face while trying to understand the native is the same confusion they face while trying to understand you. Therefore, if you cannot communicate clearly and effectively, you will never be able to share the Good News of God's love with those to whom He has sent you to minister. For this reason you must be determined that no matter what the cost in finances, time, and humiliation, you will study, learn, and practice regularly the language of your new ministry. Accept by choice that which Daniel and his three friends faced by force as they were taught the *"learning and the tongue of the Chaldeans"* (Daniel 1:1-4). Recognize that the same God, who *"did there [at Babel] confound the language of all the earth,"* is capable of helping you learn the one He wishes you to use in your ministry (Genesis 11:1-11).

Depend upon God to give you the abilities you need in His perfect timing. Accept Peter's admonition that *"if any man speak, let him speak as the oracles of God; if any man minister, let him do it as of the ability which God giveth: that God in all things may be glorified through Jesus Christ, to whom be praise and dominion for ever and ever. Amen"* (I Peter 4:11). Humbly accept that you are chosen by God, not because of your ability but rather your inability. *"For ye see your calling, brethren, how that not many wise men after the flesh, not many mighty, not many noble, are called: but God hath chosen the foolish things of the world to confound the wise; and God hath chosen the weak things of the world to confound the things which are mighty; and base things of the world, and things which are despised, hath God chosen, yea, and things which are not, to bring to nought things that are: that no flesh should glory in his presence"* (I Corinthians 1:26-29). Be humble and honest enough to say with Moses, *"O my Lord, I am not eloquent, neither heretofore, nor since thou hast spoken unto thy servant: but I am slow of speech, and of a slow tongue"* (Exodus 4:10). And then with ears of faith, hear God's encouraging response and command: *"Who hath made man's mouth? or who maketh the dumb, or deaf, or the seeing, or the blind? have not I the LORD?*

Now therefore go, and I will be with thy mouth, and teach thee what thou shalt say" (Exodus 4:11-12).

Never fall to the temptation of frustration or complacency in your language skills. But rather continually ask God to help you to improve your language abilities for the betterment of His ministry; not so that you can minister with *"excellency of speech or of wisdom"* or that your preaching is *"with enticing words of man's wisdom, but in demonstration of the Spirit and of power,"* which only comes from God (I Corinthians 2:1, 4). Then you can truly say with the Apostle Paul, *"And I, brethren, when I came to you, came not with excellency of speech or of wisdom, declaring unto you the testimony of God. For I determined not to know any thing among you, save Jesus Christ, and him crucified"* (I Corinthians 2:1-2). And then frequently ask your prayer supporters to pray *"that utterance may be given unto me [you], that I [you] may open my [your] mouth boldly, to make known the mystery of the gospel"* (Ephesians 6:19).

Actual Events

The ability to learn a language other than your own is given by God, and He alone should receive the praise and glory for any progress a missionary makes in such an endeavor. A few missionaries, such as a friend of mine, are gifted in languages and can communicate with clarity and precision. Many missionaries struggle their entire lives with failures in communication. For this reason it is very important that a missionary take time to study the native language in a specialized school or with specialized tutors

My experience in language school could be summed up in two words: "humiliation" and "Advil." This schooling was like no other I had ever encountered and became one of the most humiliating periods of my life. I found that the very gift that God had given me to communicate by spoken word in my own language was now totally set aside. Daily, even moment by moment, I was being told I was "wrong." The Advil was for the extreme headaches I had on a daily basis. I began to explain the pain as little nerves trying to tunnel new passages from one side of my brain to the other. The problem apparently was that my parents were correct when they said I had a hard head, and now the little nerves needed to constantly use dynamite in their tunneling!

I was raised on the idea that "when the going got tough, the tough got going." Sadly, as I was considering packing my bags to leave (after the first week), I needed to be reminded that this did not mean that the "tough" began running the other way but rather working harder.

Even more devastatingly, when I arrived on my field of service, I found that the nationals spoke even faster and with a more difficult accent than I ever encountered in language schooling, and the humility and headaches continued on for the first few years on the field. On many occasions I woke up in the morning looking for a reason to stay in bed so as to protect myself from my unavoidable errors, only to have my wife kindly remind me that it was Sunday (meaning, I had no choice but to once again make a public fool of myself just trying to give the hymn numbers and have the nationals look at me in total confusion). Although many missionaries have asked family and friends to pray that they would start to dream in the new language, I began to ask them to stop. I found that at times I was dreaming in my new language, but even in my dream I did not understand what was being said, so they turned into nightmares. Time after time during these first years, I was tempted by the words of one specific man who apparently enjoyed my ministry presentation and teaching while I was on deputation. The man said with all kindness and sincerity of heart, "Why are you going to be a missionary in another country and try to learn another language? You know you will never be able to communicate in that other language like you can in your own. Why are you going to set aside a gift God has given you?" The words of this kind man were not meant to build up my ego but to express the realities of language limitations. And as Satan tempted me with these frustrations, I had to make a specific choice to sacrifice my "abilities" for God's will. I needed to allow God to remove me from the equation of ministry so that, as He chose to bring success, I could not claim any for myself, because it would only be by His protection that unplanned "swearwords" written in my outline would not be spoken from the pulpit while I was preaching on the very subject of proper communication (p.s. the dictionary didn't tell me it was a bad word in my country). So, as I continue to find myself being corrected and asking nationals to repeat themselves for clarification, I must still trust God to work through my limitations for His glory. The frustration of not being understood and of not understanding others in critical moments of life and ministry must be calmed by the faith that God is at work both *for* me and *through* me even when I lack understanding, because *"his ways [are] past finding out!"* (Romans 11:33).

Biblical Exhortation

Dear servant of God, you must not be consumed by your language ability or lack of thereof. With each mistake you make, dedicate yourself to never quit the learning process, and ask God Who has formed your mouth, tongue, and ears to provide the clarity you need (Exodus 4:11). And when confusion comes, you must not become overcome with despair, but rather have faith that God is never confused. Because He is your Guide for all of life and ministry, you will face no damage or success that He has not perfectly approved. Allow the thorn of communication to be a protection from ever becoming *"exalted above measure"* (II Corinthians 12:7).

Practical Participation

✎ **Missionary Candidate - Please prepare** properly by taking time (even years) to study the language of your future ministry. Always depend upon the God Who created all languages to give you the clarity needed to accomplish His work for the people to whom He has called you to minister. Ask Him to help you master the "love language" of the nationals so that you can share His love with them. And never cheat yourself and those you serve by being complacent or prideful in your language skills.

✎ **Missionary's Supporter - Please pray** for the missionary as he enters a very confusing world. Request God's protection from those who would seek to take advantage of his limited language skills. Ask God to provide others who know his language who can be true helpers in the adjusting and learning process. Then pray that his mind, mouth, and ears would be opened to truly communicate with very little distractions, so that the Gospel would not be hindered. **Please provide** him with the assurance of your prayers for this specific need, and be faithful to pray for clear communication during services and ministry opportunities. Provide words both in writing and in conversation that will be comforting, encouraging, and refreshing. Your words may be the only ones he has truly understood all day long. And provide him the time he needs to properly prepare himself for his new life and ministry through language and cultural studies.

✎ **Missionary in Service - Please press on** by accepting that God has created you with the specific language abilities He knew you would need to accomplish the ministry He has called you to. Do not allow the corrections and even criticisms of others to discourage you from seeing God's strength displayed in your weakness. And never let the learning process end. Constantly ask God to improve your ability to communicate His Gospel to the lost and His spiritual truths to the saved.

Increase Your Faith

Exodus 4:10-12
10 And Moses said unto the LORD,
O my Lord, I am not eloquent, neither heretofore,
nor since thou hast spoken unto thy servant:
but I am slow of speech, and of a slow tongue.
11 And the LORD said unto him,
Who hath made man's mouth?
or who maketh the dumb, or deaf,
or the seeing, or the blind?
have not I the LORD?
12 Now therefore go, and I will be with thy mouth,
and teach thee what thou shalt say.

I Corinthians 1:26-29
26 For ye see your calling, brethren,
how that not many wise men after the flesh,
not many mighty, not many noble, are called:
27 But God hath chosen the foolish things of the world
to confound the wise;
and God hath chosen the weak things of the world
to confound the things which are mighty;
28 And base things of the world,
and things which are despised, hath God chosen,
yea, and things which are not,
to bring to nought things that are:
29 That no flesh should glory in his presence.

I Corinthians 2:1-5

*1 And I, brethren, when I came to you,
came not with excellency of speech or of wisdom,
declaring unto you the testimony of God.
2 For I determined not to know any thing among you,
save Jesus Christ, and him crucified.
3 And I was with you in weakness,
and in fear, and in much trembling.
4 And my speech and my preaching
was not with enticing words of man's wisdom,
but in demonstration of the Spirit and of power:
5 That your faith should not stand in the wisdom of men,
but in the power of God.*

Ephesians 6:18-20

*18 Praying always
with all prayer and supplication in the Spirit,
and watching thereunto
with all perseverance and supplication for all saints;
19 And for me, that utterance may be given unto me,
that I may open my mouth boldly,
to make known the mystery of the gospel,
20 For which I am an ambassador in bonds:
that therein I may speak boldly, as I ought to speak.*

I Peter 4:10-11

*10 As every man hath received the gift,
even so minister the same one to another,
as good stewards of the manifold grace of God.
11 If any man speak, let him speak as the oracles of God;
if any man minister,
let him do it as of the ability which God giveth:
that God in all things may be glorified through Jesus Christ,
to whom be praise and dominion for ever and ever. Amen.*

Romans 10:17

*So then faith cometh by hearing,
and hearing by the word of God.*

Examples of Like Faith

Joseph
Genesis 37:23-28, Psalm 81:5

Jeremiah
Jeremiah 1:4-10

Romans 15:4
For whatsoever things were written aforetime
were written for our learning,
that we through patience and comfort of the scriptures
might have hope.

Chapter 5

FINAL DESTINATION

II Thessalonians 3:1-2
Finally, brethren, pray for us,
that the word of the Lord may have free course, and be glorified,
even as it is with you:
and that we may be delivered
from unreasonable and wicked men:
for all men have not faith

The Missionary's Experience

After arriving in his new country and getting through the process of gathering his belongings from the airport, the missionary begins the journey to his final destination for the day. Although he may be looking forward to the opportunity to rest and settle in for the evening, he may find that his attention is drawn to the real meaning of the words "final destination." He may even begin to believe that his final destination for that day is also his "final destination" for all eternity. With that in mind, he is so tempted to ask the driver to return him to the airport. He may even begin to consider telling the driver that he lost something precious, something he is sure he will never find in this new country, "his security." These thoughts are brought about by simple observation of the driving habits (if his eyes are still open) that do not resemble any level of order. He may even begin to consider the parable of the "good Samaritan" (Luke 10:25-37) because he is noticing what appear to be criminals and vagabonds lurking on every corner. He is sure they would not think twice about robbing him of all of his belongings and even his life. With his sense of self-protection heightened, he breathes a small sigh of relief as the driver pulls up to that physical place of rest for the night and says, "We are here." However, his "level of alert" is only lowered from RED to ORANGE as he notices that the house in front of him looks more like a prison than anything else. The sturdy locked gate around the property, bars on the windows, the extra locks on the doors—all of which are to provide security—actually provide a feeling of insecurity. Over the next few weeks and months, he finds that his initial concerns about his security were quite valid, as he sees firsthand the results of poverty, greed, crime, drugs, etc. Even more devastatingly, he notices that the police force has no enforcement. And as he begins to learn more about the people God has called him to serve, by reading newspapers and hearing news reports, he finds that the nationals live in the same fear that he does. And so his suspicions have been confirmed, he has truly lost his "security" and will not find it again anytime soon.

Biblical Examples

Dear servant of God, you must not shrink from these dangers. The Apostle Paul faced such dangers. He knew the dangers of ministering around the world. He shared with the church at Corinth that he was "*in labours more abundant, in stripes above measure, in prisons more frequent, in deaths oft. Of the Jews five times received I forty stripes save one. Thrice was I beaten with rods, once was I stoned, thrice I suffered shipwreck, a night and a day I have been in the deep; in journeyings often, in perils of waters, in perils of robbers, in perils by mine own countrymen, in perils by the heathen, in perils in the city, in perils in the wilderness, in perils in the sea, in perils among false brethren; in weariness and painfulness, in watchings often, in hunger and thirst, in fastings often, in cold and nakedness*" (II Corinthians 11:23-27). For this very reason he said to the believers in Thessalonica, "*Finally, brethren, pray for us, that the word of the Lord may have free course, and be glorified, even as it is with you: and that we may be delivered from unreasonable and wicked men: for all men have not faith*" (II Thessalonians 3:1-2).

Do not kid yourself, the dangers that surround you are real and cannot be denied! Therefore, be very careful to not exaggerate nor diminish them with flowery spiritual words as you speak to those who care about you and pray for you. Rather say with the Apostle Paul, *"For we would not, brethren, have you ignorant of our trouble which came [is coming] to us"* (II Corinthians 1:8), and then ask others to face these dangers with you by praying for you regularly, as well as in any moments that the Holy Spirit brings you specifically to mind. Take heed that you are not overcome by these fears, but remember that *"the wicked flee when no man pursueth: but the righteous are bold as a lion"* (I Peter 1:13). *"For God hath not given us the spirit of fear; but of power, and of love, and of a sound mind"* (II Timothy 1:7).

Begin to depend on God's promise that *"the angel of the LORD encampeth round about them that fear him, and delivereth them"* (Psalm 34:7, II Kings 6:14-23). Take heart that as Job's family nor possessions could be touched by Satan without permission from God, so God holds you in His protective hand (Job 1:1-2:8).

Determine to follow Job's example, when God does permit dangers to touch your life, as he *"arose, and rent his mantle, and shaved his head, and fell down upon the ground, and worshipped, and said, Naked came I out of my mother's womb, and naked shall I return thither: the LORD gave, and the LORD hath taken away; blessed be the name of the LORD. In all this Job sinned not, nor charged God foolishly."* God said, *"I will never leave thee, nor forsake thee. So that we may boldly say, The Lord is my helper, and I will not fear what man shall do unto me"* (Hebrews 13:5-6). As your all-loving God wisely chooses for you to be touched by the wicked actions of those around you, follow the example of the saints of faith found in Hebrews 11:33-39, *"who through faith subdued kingdoms, wrought righteousness, obtained promises, stopped the mouths of lions, quenched the violence of fire, escaped the edge of the sword, out of weakness were made strong, waxed valiant in fight, turned to flight the armies of the aliens. Women received their dead raised to life again: and others were tortured, not accepting deliverance; that they might obtain a better resurrection: and others had trial of cruel mockings and scourgings, yea, moreover of bonds and imprisonment: they were stoned, they were sawn asunder, were tempted, were slain with the sword: they wandered about in sheepskins and goatskins; being destitute, afflicted, tormented; (of whom the world was not worthy:) they wandered in deserts, and in mountains, and in dens and caves of the earth. And these all, having obtained a good report through faith, received not the promise."*

Finally, dedicate yourself to *"love your enemies, bless them that curse you, do good to them that hate you, and pray for them which despitefully use you, and persecute you"* (Matthew 5:44). You must see the very actions against others and even yourself as evidence of their need of your presence. You must *"do all things without murmurings and disputings: That ye may be blameless and harmless, the sons of God, without rebuke, in the midst of a crooked and perverse nation, among whom ye shine as lights in the world; holding forth the word of life"* (Philippians 2:14-16). For *"ye are the light of the world. . . . Let your light so shine before men, that they may see your good works, and glorify your Father which is in heaven"* (Matthew 5:14-16). Fulfill your calling as a missionary *"to open their eyes, and to turn them from darkness to light, and from the power of Satan unto God, that they may receive forgiveness of sins, and inheritance among them which are sanctified by faith that is in me [Jesus Christ]"* (Acts 26:18). Do not shrink back from the dangers, but face each one with godly confidence knowing that *"in all these things we are more than conquerors through him that loved us. For I [you] am [should be] persuaded, that neither death, nor life, nor angels, nor principalities, nor powers, nor things present, nor things to come, nor height, nor depth, nor any other creature, shall be able to separate us [you] from the love of God, which is in Christ Jesus our Lord"* (Romans 8:38-39).

Actual Events

Each missionary enters his own set of dangers. Each country around the world maintains a different standard of morality and civility. However, I share these Biblical truths with you because I have faced the choice of hating or loving the very people to whom

God has sent me to minister. It was within less than one month following my arrival on my field of service that my temporary residence (the second floor of our church building) was robbed two times and some of my precious and personal possessions were stolen. The thieves had the audacity not only to liberate me of my belongings but also to eat out of my fridge (ice cream, of all things) and to steal my baby's jars of food. Then, the day following the second theft, I watched a man walk down the street wearing my T-shirt. The rage set in, and the anger flared, but thankfully there was nothing I could do. When I asked other missionaries about calling the police, I was told it would be a waste of time, and so I had no choice but to leave it with the Lord. I was forced to follow Paul's command in Romans 12:19 which says, *"Dearly beloved, avenge not yourselves, but rather give place unto wrath: for it is written, Vengeance is mine; I will repay, saith the Lord."*

For days and weeks following the robberies, I found my three-year-old son hiding things under his bed. When I asked him about what he was doing, he said he didn't want the bad men to get them. As parents, my wife and I, with broken hearts, encouraged him with Psalm 53:6, which a precious teacher had taught him while we were in language school, *"What time I am afraid, I will trust in thee."* Three months later, as I waited at our church meeting place for others to show up for visitation, I heard five gunshots, and a short time later I found myself standing in the middle of the road with a crowd of people (I could not understand) as the police collected the body of the man who had been murdered. Once again, danger and death surrounded me, but I had no choice but to carry on in the faith that my life would not be touched until God permitted. A short time later, while distributing tracts house to house with two teenage nationals, they refused to get out of the car in one area of town in the middle of the day. When I asked them about their refusal, they informed me that they knew this area of town and knew the danger. So, while harassing them for being chickens, I also encouraged my heart by sharing with them that no one could bring us harm without God's permission. I exited the car (while they stayed inside with doors closed tight) and finished the task with not one hint of danger. Many more personal stories could be told, and many other missionaries have much greater personal testimonies of God's protective hand.

Biblical Exhortation

Dear servant of God, a story told of the past often confuses God as the God only of the past, but God is the God of the present. You must enter whatever danger that may await you saying with David as he was confronted with the great danger from Goliath, *"Is there not a cause?"* (I Samuel 17:29). The answer is a resounding "YES." The cause is CHRIST. Make Paul's testimony your own as he said, *"Notwithstanding the Lord stood with me, and strengthened me; that by me the preaching might be fully known, and that all the Gentiles might hear: and I was delivered out of the mouth of the lion. And the Lord shall deliver me from every evil work, and will preserve me unto his heavenly kingdom: to whom be glory for ever and ever. Amen"* (II Timothy 4:17-18). Begin each day realizing that your personal safety does not rest in your strength or your surroundings but in your Savior. Depend on His promise that He *"will never leave thee, nor forsake thee. So that we may boldly say, The Lord is my helper, and I will not fear what man shall do unto me"* (Hebrews 13:5b-6). As real dangers present themselves, do not deny their existence, for *"a prudent man foreseeth the evil, and hideth [protects] himself: but the simple pass on, and are punished"* (Proverbs 22:3). Pray with the saints of the early church, *"Grant unto thy servants, that with all boldness they may speak thy word"* (Acts 4:29). *"For God hath not given us the spirit of fear; but of power, and of love, and of a sound mind"* (II Timothy 1:7).

Practical Participation

✎ **Missionary Candidate - Please prepare** yourself for the realistic dangers and trials that you may face in your service as one of God's soldiers on the front lines of the battle. You must remember that there is no war without wounds and prepare your spiritual first aid kit so that you are not defeated in the battle. Prepare most of all with confidence in your Commander and Chief, your Heavenly Father, and fill your heart and mind with those passages that will assure you of His protection, according to His perfect love and will for you personally.

✎ **Missionary's Supporter - Please pray** for the safety of the missionary as he is confronted with dangers and diseases that could bring his ministry to an early end. Pray for God's constant provision of wisdom and power in each and every situation in which the missionary may find himself. When the missionary is brought to your mind at an unplanned time, pray earnestly for whatever need he may be facing at that very moment, while realizing that you may very well be part of God's perfect provision of safety during life-threatening events. **Please provide** sufficiently for the missionary to be able to maintain a secure environment for himself, family, and ministry. Please be a kind and sympathetic ear when he shares his safety concerns, and realize that although you may have seen such needs in the news, these dangers are real and constant burdens the missionary must personally guard against on a daily bases.

✎ **Missionary in Service - Please press on** by trusting God to provide His protection while you continue to serve Him with your life as a light in the dark. Press on in your work of carrying the Gospel to those who are living in the same dangers you are experiencing. Continue to share the true hope that Jesus Christ is the only answer to remove these dangers and only consolation when victims' lives are touched by these dangers.

Increase Your Faith

Psalm 56:3

3 What time I am afraid, I will trust in thee.

Luke 12:4-5

4 And I say unto you my friends,
Be not afraid of them that kill the body,
and after that have no more that they can do.
5 But I will forewarn you whom ye shall fear:
Fear him, which after he hath killed
hath power to cast into hell;
yea, I say unto you, Fear him.

Acts 20:14

24 But none of these things move me,
neither count I my life dear unto myself,
so that I might finish my course with joy, and the ministry,
which I have received of the Lord Jesus,
to testify the gospel of the grace of God.

Romans 8:35-39

35 Who shall separate us from the love of Christ?
shall tribulation, or distress, or persecution,
or famine, or nakedness, or peril, or sword?
36 As it is written, For thy sake we are killed all the day long;
we are accounted as sheep for the slaughter.
37 Nay, in all these things we are more than conquerors
through him that loved us.
38 For I am persuaded, that neither death, nor life,
nor angels, nor principalities, nor powers,
nor things present, nor things to come,
39 Nor height, nor depth, nor any other creature,
shall be able to separate us from the love of God,
which is in Christ Jesus our Lord.

II Timothy 4:17-18

17 Notwithstanding the Lord stood with me,
and strengthened me;
that by me the preaching might be fully known,
and that all the Gentiles might hear:
and I was delivered out of the mouth of the lion.
18 And the Lord shall deliver me from every evil work,
and will preserve me unto his heavenly kingdom:
to whom be glory for ever and ever. Amen.

Hebrews 13:5-6

5 Let your conversation be without covetousness;
and be content with such things as ye have: for he hath said,
I will never leave thee, nor forsake thee.
6 So that we may boldly say,
The Lord is my helper,
and I will not fear what man shall do unto me.

Romans 10:17
So then faith cometh by hearing,
and hearing by the word of God.

Examples of Like Faith

David
I Samuel 17:1-58

Shadrach, Meshach, and Abednego
Daniel 3:1-30

Daniel
Daniel 6:1-28

Paul
Acts 14:18-21, 19:23-20:1,
I Corinthians 15:32, II Corinthians 1:3-11

Saints of Faith
Hebrews 11:33-40

Romans 15:4
For whatsoever things were written aforetime
were written for our learning,
that we through patience and comfort of the scriptures
might have hope.

Chapter 6

THE DARKNESS OF SIN

Acts 26:18
To open their eyes, and to turn them from darkness to light,
and from the power of Satan unto God,
that they may receive forgiveness of sins,
and inheritance among them which are sanctified
by faith that is in me.

The Missionary's Experience

The missionary who has dedicated his life to share *"the light of the glorious gospel of Christ"* with those who walk in darkness will often find himself in some of the most spiritually dark places in the world (II Corinthians 4:4). No matter if he is serving in the most luxurious mansions or the poorest huts, he will often sense the depths of sin's dark depravity all around him. Sin's depravity may be displayed in many public ways, such as open sensuality, drunkenness, thefts, etc., or it may work privately or publicly through false religions and satanic worship. With these influences all around him, the missionary will at times almost physically feel the spiritual coldness closing in around him as he attempts to minister to those who have never experienced the warmth of God's light through Jesus Christ. Often, as he seeks to share the light of Jesus Christ with those in such darkness, he will find that those who are lost enjoy their condition, while those who are saved enjoy the guarantee of eternal life in heaven but want very little to do with the full impact of God's light of truth reaching the deep, dark areas of their own hearts here on earth. It is during these moments of spiritual conflict between light and darkness that the missionary will have but one hope: his faith that he serves an all-powerful God, Who "*is light, and in him is no darkness at all*" (I John 1:5).

Biblical Examples

Dear servant of God, the darkness around you is real. Those who live in such sinful surroundings face the realistic possibility of spiritual destruction, just as Lot did. The difference is made in whether or not you will continue to reveal your light, or if you will choose to be like Lot and place your light under a bushel. Lot chose to be "*vexed with the filthy conversation of the wicked: (For that righteous man dwelling among them, in seeing and hearing, vexed his righteous soul from day to day with their unlawful deeds)*," but he never chose to repel the darkness with the light of truth (II Peter 2:7-8). Rather, he embraced it as the norm for himself and his family (Genesis 19:1). Lot's acceptance of the spiritual darkness was clearly revealed as he said to the men of Sodom, "*I have two daughters which have not known man; let me, I pray you, bring them out unto you, and do ye to them as is good in your eyes*" (Genesis 19:8). The sad conclusion to Lot's time in the darkness of Sodom is shown as two angels "*said unto Lot, Hast thou here any besides? son in law, and thy sons, and thy daughters, and whatsoever thou hast in the city, bring them out of this place: For we will destroy this place, because the cry of them is waxen great before the face of the LORD; and the LORD hath sent us to destroy it. And Lot went out, and spake unto his sons in law, which married his daughters, and said, Up, get you out of this place; for the LORD will destroy this city. But he seemed as one that mocked unto his sons in law. And when the morning arose, then the angels hastened Lot, saying, Arise, take thy wife, and thy two daughters, which are here; lest thou be consumed in the iniquity of the city. And while he lingered, the men laid hold upon his hand, and upon the hand of his wife, and upon the hand of his two daughters; the LORD being merciful unto him: and they brought him forth, and set him without the city*" (Genesis 19:12-17).

Lot and his family were so influenced by the spiritual darkness of their surroundings that his daughters and sons-in-law mocked him, and he, his wife, and his two virgin daughters were forced out of the city against their will by the two angels. This is the same danger that each man, woman, and child faces every day as they live in a spiritually dark environment—the danger of accepting the darkness as being all right and thereby rejecting God's confrontation and protection when He offers it. For this reason, Paul shares God's standard and promise for separation from the world by saying "*Be ye not unequally yoked together with unbelievers: for what fellowship hath righteousness with unrighteousness? and what communion hath light with darkness? And what concord hath Christ with Belial? or what part hath he that believeth with an infidel? And what agreement hath the temple of God with idols? for ye are the temple of the living God; as God hath said, I will dwell in them, and walk in them; and I will be their God, and they shall be my people. Wherefore come out from among them, and be ye separate, saith the Lord, and touch not the unclean thing; and I will receive you, and will be a Father unto you, and ye shall be my sons and daughters, saith the Lord Almighty*" (II Corinthians 6:14-18).

Actual Events

Joseph provides a clear example of living in the midst of a wicked environment without allowing it to dwell in him. Having the responsibility of running Potiphar's business and home, he was also subject to the spiritual wickedness of Potiphar's wife, who "*cast her eyes upon Joseph; and she said, Lie with me. But he refused, and said . . . how then can I do this great wickedness, and sin against God?*" (Genesis 39:7-9). But Potiphar's wife was persistent, and "*she spake to Joseph day by day, that he hearkened not unto her, to lie by her, or to be with her*" (Genesis 39:10). Joseph, although he was required to work in a spiritually dangerous environment, sought to protect himself from its temptations by avoiding Potiphar's wife. However, she sought an opportunity and entrapped him. Even with a clear opportunity to give in to the influences of sin, he did not; "*he left his garment in her hand, and fled, and got him out*" (Genesis

39:12). Joseph did not allow the wicked society of Egypt, the reality that he was far away from family and friends and dwelling among strangers, or the constant bombardment and specific invitation for sin to destroy his dedication to God.

The believers in Ephesus also lived in a world of darkness. Their city was known for its worship of the goddess Diana to the extent that the people tried kill Paul for preaching Jesus Christ (Acts 19:22-41, I Corinthians 15:32). In this very culture and environment, new believers were so committed to remove spiritual darkness from their lives and homes that *"many that believed came, and confessed, and shewed their deeds. Many of them also which used curious arts brought their books together, and burned them before all men: and they counted the price of them, and found it fifty thousand pieces of silver. So mightily grew the word of God and prevailed"* (Acts 19:18-20). The spiritual darkness around us is not to be given in to or feared but rather to serve as a constant reminder of our responsibility – our responsibility to be *"the light of the world"* (Matthew 5:14) and to *"let your [our] light so shine before men, that they may see your [our] good works, and glorify your [our] Father which is in heaven"* (Matthew 5:16).

While on deputation, a guest speaker at one of our mission's conferences spoke to me about his experience years earlier while he was a missionary in the same country to which I was planning to go. He shared with me that he had never before experienced the extreme spiritual pressure he had felt from the moment he arrived in the country until he left years later to return to his homeland. He said it was physically draining and spiritually discouraging. I can personally attest to this man's experience. The seemingly constant pressure can be overwhelming, and yet there is often no real logical reason that can be found. Perhaps it is the constant spiritual battle of preventing the sensuality and lewdness to become part of my life. Perhaps it is the pressure of dealing with those who are hurting because they have lived in spiritual darkness for so long and now are reaping the fruit of their sin. Or perhaps even more difficult are those who do not want to change but rather enjoy their wickedness even while still claiming to be Christians. Maybe it is the reality that next to my church building we have practicing spiritists (voodoo worshipers) who meet regularly. Whatever the case, the pressure of sin's darkness is constantly real. For this reason, I find hope in one thing: that I am *"of God, little children, and have overcome them: because greater is he that is in you [me], than he that is in the world"* (I John 4:4). *"For whatsoever is born of God overcometh the world: and this is the victory that overcometh the world, even our faith. Who is he that overcometh the world, but he that believeth that Jesus is the Son of God"* (I John 5:4-5).

Biblical Exhortation

Dear servant of God, you must constantly remember that the very reason you are called to be a missionary is so you can share the light of Jesus Christ with those entrapped by Satan's darkness. You must always remember that *"if our gospel be hid, it is hid to them that are lost: in whom the god of this world hath blinded the minds of them which believe not, lest the light of the glorious gospel of Christ, who is the image of God, should shine unto them"* (II Corinthians 4:3-4). For this reason, you must dedicate yourself to never allow your light to flicker or fail. You must remember that the ministry you are fulfilling is a direct attack on the sin nature of man and Satan, who encourages it.

You must not be surprised when men love their *"darkness rather than light, because their deeds were evil. For every one that doeth evil hateth the light, neither cometh to the light, lest his deeds should be reproved. But he that doeth truth cometh to the light, that his deeds may be made manifest, that they are wrought in God"* (John 3:19-21). However, as you live among those who enjoy the darkness of their sin, you must not allow your life to be affected by that same darkness. You must remember that, as God's child, *"ye are all the children of light, and the children of the day: we are not of the night, nor of darkness. Therefore let us not sleep, as do others; but let us watch and be sober. For they that sleep sleep in the night; and they that be drunken are drunken in the night. But let us, who are of the day, be sober, putting on the breastplate of faith and love; and for an helmet, the hope of salvation"* (I Thessalonians 5:5-8). You must take the warning to not be *"deceived: evil communications corrupt good manners. Awake to righteousness, and sin not; for some have not the knowledge of God: I speak this to your shame"* (I Corinthians 15:33-34).

As you rub shoulders with the darkness of sin every day, you must remember to *"love not the world, neither the things that are in the world. If any man love the world, the love of the Father is not in him. For all that is in the world, the lust of the flesh, and the lust of the eyes, and the pride of life, is not of the Father, but is of the world"* (I John 2:15-16). *"And be not conformed to this world: but be ye transformed by the renewing of your mind, that ye may prove what is that good, and acceptable, and perfect, will of God"* (Romans 12:2). Be sure to be constantly *"building up yourselves on your most holy faith, praying in the Holy Ghost, keep yourselves in the love of God, looking for the mercy of our Lord Jesus Christ unto eternal life. And of some have compassion, making a difference: and others save with fear, pulling them out of the fire; hating even the garment spotted by the flesh"* (Jude 1:20-23). While you perform this most noble and necessary task in the midst of sin's darkness, you must commit yourself and your loved ones *"unto him that is able to keep you from falling, and to present you faultless before the presence of his glory with exceeding joy, to the only wise God our Saviour, be glory and majesty, dominion and power, both now and ever. Amen"* (Jude 1:24-25).

Practical Participation

✎ **Missionary Candidate - Please prepare** for the spiritual battles and temptation you will face as you live and work in a sin-filled environment. Make sure you are grounded in God's holiness and that you regularly ask God to show you areas of your life that must be confessed as sin. Prepare yourself by finding other believers who love you and who will encourage you to not become as the world around you but will instead challenge you to continue to be a brilliant light representing the Gospel.

✎ **Missionary's Supporter - Please pray** regularly and earnestly for the spiritual protection of your missionary. Please pray that he will not become accustomed to sin but rather will continually find God's Word as the standard for right and wrong and live in accordance to what is right. **Please provide** him with encouraging words and materials that will help him to stay focused on God's holiness and his task of sharing that holiness with the world around him. Provide him with encouraging words when he is struggling under the heavy weight of spiritual attacks affecting his health, attitude, and courage to continue.

✎ **Missionary in Service - Please press on** in the midst of the darkness, knowing that you have been sent by the God of light to share His Gospel Light with those in darkness. Please press on without permitting the darkness to infiltrate and destroy your light. Continually return to God's Word so that it might be the lamp that lights your path and keeps you reflecting its light throughout your daily life and ministry (Psalm 119:105).

Increase Your Faith

Psalm 119:105

*105 Thy word is a lamp unto my feet,
and a light unto my path.*

John 8:12

*12 Then spake Jesus again unto them, saying,
I am the light of the world:
he that followeth me shall not walk in darkness,
but shall have the light of life.*

John 17:14-17

*14 I have given them thy word;
and the world hath hated them,
because they are not of the world,
even as I am not of the world.
15 I pray not that thou shouldest take them out of the world,
but that thou shouldest keep them from the evil.
16 They are not of the world,
even as I am not of the world.
17 Sanctify them through thy truth: thy word is truth.*

Romans 12:1-2

*1 I beseech you therefore, brethren, by the mercies of God,
that ye present your bodies a living sacrifice,
holy, acceptable unto God,
which is your reasonable service.
2 And be not conformed to this world:
but be ye transformed by the renewing of your mind,
that ye may prove what is that good
and acceptable, and perfect,
will of God.*

Ephesians 5:8-16

8 For ye were sometimes darkness,
but now are ye light in the Lord:
walk as children of light:
9 (For the fruit of the Spirit
is in all goodness and righteousness and truth;)
10 Proving what is acceptable unto the Lord.
11 And have no fellowship
with the unfruitful works of darkness,
but rather reprove them.
12 For it is a shame even to speak
of those things which are done of them in secret.
13 But all things that are reproved
are made manifest by the light:
for whatsoever doth make manifest is light.
14 Wherefore he saith, Awake thou that sleepest,
and arise from the dead, and Christ shall give thee light.
15 See then that ye walk circumspectly,
not as fools, but as wise,
16 Redeeming the time, because the days are evil.

II Peter 1:19

19 We have also a more sure word of prophecy;
whereunto ye do well that ye take heed,
as unto a light that shineth in a dark place,
until the day dawn, and the day star arise in your hearts:

I John 4:4

4 Ye are of God, little children,
and have overcome them:
because greater is he that is in you,
than he that is in the world.

Romans 10:17

So then faith cometh by hearing,
and hearing by the word of God.

Examples of Like Faith

Noah
Genesis 6:1-13

Paul
Acts 17:16-34

The Church in Pergamos
Revelation 2:12-17

Romans 15:4
For whatsoever things were written aforetime
were written for our learning,
that we through patience and comfort of the scriptures
might have hope.

Chapter 7

THE FILTH OF THIS WORLD

Mark 7:2, 15
And when they saw some of his disciples eat bread with defiled,
that is to say, with unwashen, hands, they found fault.
There is nothing from without a man,
that entering into him can defile him:
but the things which come out of him,
those are they that defile the man.

The Missionary's Experience

Within the first moments after the missionary arrives in his new country, he will most likely notice that the standard for cleanliness is much different than that of his mother's. Although the initial shock of these differences may be suppressed by his confusion in his new surroundings, the filth of this world, found in the dirty streets, unpleasant smells, un-kept stores, restaurants and public bathrooms, as well as the personal hygiene of the nationals he encounters in the first few days and weeks, may quickly draw his attention to his own personal health. He may even begin to carry a bottle of hand sanitizer (if he can find any) in his pocket and sneak a little after each hand shake or door he opens, not due to his fear of the common cold, but rather of a life-altering disease. If this were not enough, he receives very specific warning from fellow missionaries or even nationals about the drinking water and the symptoms of local illnesses and diseases. At the smallest turn of his stomach or extra bead of perspiration on his forehead, he quickly does an entire body exam to reassure himself that he is not, within his first year on the field, becoming one of those old, sickly missionaries he had heard of.

Biblical Examples

Dear servant of God, have you considered the utter filth-, germ-, and bug-infested environment in which Paul and Silas found themselves as they sat in the jail in Philippi with open wounds from having been beaten and how they *"prayed, and sang praises unto God"* so that *"the prisoners heard them"* and that God caused a *"great earthquake, so that the foundations of the prison were shaken"* (Acts 16:23-26)? Or have you considered the mucky and muddy hole in which Jeremiah was placed for preaching God's message (Jeremiah 38:1-9)? Jeremiah 38:6 says, *"There was no water, but mire: so Jeremiah sunk in the mire."* Jeremiah's condition was so disgusting that *"the king commanded Ebedmelech the Ethiopian, saying, Take from hence thirty men with thee, and take up Jeremiah the prophet out of the dungeon, before he die. So Ebedmelech took the men with him, and went into the house of the king under the treasury, and took thence old cast clouts and old rotten rags, and let them down by cords into the dungeon to Jeremiah. And Ebedmelech the Ethiopian said unto Jeremiah, Put now these old cast clouts and rotten rags under thine armholes under the cords. And Jeremiah did so. So they drew up Jeremiah with cords, and took him up out of the dungeon"* (Jeremiah 38:10-13). Even after such an experience, Jeremiah continued to proclaim the true words of God throughout the rest of his life and ministry. Most of all, it would be beneficial to consider the example of our Lord, as He placed Himself in a position of a servant in order to clean the dirtiest part of His disciples' bodies—their feet. John 13:4-5 says, *"He riseth from supper, and laid aside his garments; and took a towel, and girded himself. After that he poureth water into a bason, and began to wash the disciples' feet, and to wipe them with the towel wherewith he was girded."* Jesus, the Creator of all, the Holy One, was willing to make Himself lower than a servant by touching and cleaning the disciples' dirty feet, and then He followed His humble actions by saying, *"Know ye what I have done to you? Ye call me Master and Lord: and ye say well; for so I am. If I then, your Lord and Master, have washed your feet; ye also ought to wash one another's feet. For I have given you an example, that ye should do as I have done to you.*" In essence, Jesus was teaching His disciples that if they were not willing to humbly serve each other and others in their dirtiest of conditions, they were not truly His followers.

Actual Events

Many missionaries who visit and survey their field of service before moving there often look through the eyes of a tourist and therefore overlook much of the grit and grime of their future homeland. This was my experience on my first visit to my country of service. I was a teenager, and I really paid little attention to the litter or the number of overflowing trash cans in the streets. But as God provided me more opportunities to visit, these environmental realities began to sink in. On one of my trips, I remember specifically asking my wife if the country had always been so dirty or if I was just noticing it more. Thankfully, for me, by the time we moved to live and serve as missionaries in our field of service, I was well aware of many of the unsanitary conditions in which we would be living. One of the experiences that had prepared me was a visit to a Burger King bathroom. Of course I had been in dirty bathrooms before. I had even worked on fixing bathrooms with plumbing problems and had visited a waste water treatment plant where my father had worked when I was a child (providing me ample experiences of horrific sights and smells). But the smells and sights of this particular bathroom, in which toilet paper was not permitted to be flushed, where the trash can was overflowing, and the wet floor was assumedly caused by a plumbing problem, were just a bit overwhelming. But there seemed to be no alarm to those in charge or reason for the restaurant to make repairs. This condition was the norm. As I moved to live and minister in a "civilized" country, I was often reminded that the definition of "civilized" is subjective. One very disturbing truth about the country in which I live is that of the existence, size, and commonality of cockroaches. Having grown up in a city with row-homes, I was accustomed to the need for exterminating services in one's home on a monthly basis to remove these unwanted, germ-carrying, night-crawling pests. But I was NOT accustomed to needing extermination services for one's car, as well. But the thought of driving down the road with a roach crawling up my leg was simply not going to be an option. One evening, as my son climbed into another missionary's car, he mentioned that he saw a roach. Without hesitation, anxiety, or shame, the missionary simply replied by saying, "Yup, not much you can do about that; they get in everywhere." On another particular occasion, I was contacted by a man who was house-bound due to illness. When I went to visit him in his home, I nearly choked at the condition in which he lived. He asked me to bring my church members (women and children included) to visit him, and I needed to catch myself from verbally shrieking. However, while visiting with him and taking note of some of the open sores on his feet, I was reminded of the willingness of Jesus Christ, my Lord and Example, to minister to those who had dirty feet. I was reminded of the care of the Good Samaritan in comparison to the phony religion of the priest and Levite.

Biblical Exhortation

Dear servant of God, your health is of the utmost importance, for without it, you cannot do the work of the ministry. But you must not fear those things which you cannot see, such as germs, because of the dirtiness you can see. You must recognize that man has been living on this dirty earth since creation and that God created our bodies to repel most of the germs found in the average dirty environment. You must be willing to go where God sends you, no matter what the physical conditions. Of course you must be prudent. Just as a fireman does not enter a burning building without proper protection, you must take those protective measures available to you to protect your health. At the same time, you must not neglect to enter those environments that seem "un-healthy" simply because you are uncomfortable. You must trust God to be your ultimate protector, and you must reach those to whom He has called you to minister no matter what condition of life you find them in. You must remember *"there is nothing from without a man, that entering into him can defile him: but the things which come out of him, those are they that defile the man"* (Mark 7:15).

Practical Participation

✎ **Missionary Candidate** - **Please prepare** yourself physically for any known sanitary concerns you may encounter on your field of service. Prepare yourself spiritually by participating in any ministry opportunity God provides you, no matter how dirty it may be.

✎ **Missionary's Supporter** - **Please pray** for your missionary, for he must enter streets, homes, and hospitals full of dangerous germs, which could cause him serious sickness and even death. Please pray for him to never shrink back from reaching those who live in such filthy conditions but rather that they would share the love of God without hesitation. **Please provide** for them the necessary supplies and equipment so that they can take the appropriate precautions needed to prevent unnecessary sickness due to filthy water, food, etc. Also, provide for them to receive the rest and proper treatment when they do fall sick because of the germs they have encountered while fulfilling their ministry for the Lord.

✎ **Missionary in Service** - **Please press on** no matter the environment in which you find yourself. Recognize that your Creator is also your Sustainer, and depend on Him for protection from any illnesses or diseases you may be introduced to because of your ministry. Please press on even when the very sights, smells, and sounds turn your stomach and break your heart, so that you can share the love of God with those who live in those conditions on a daily basis.

Increase Your Faith

Mark 7:18-23

18 And he saith unto them,
Are ye so without understanding also?
Do ye not perceive,
that whatsoever thing from without entereth into the man,
it cannot defile him;
19 Because it entereth not into his heart,
but into the belly,
and goeth out into the draught, purging all meats?
20 And he said, That which cometh out of the man,
that defileth the man.
21 For from within, out of the heart of men,
proceed evil thoughts, adulteries, fornications, murders,
22 Thefts, covetousness, wickedness, deceit, lasciviousness,
an evil eye, blasphemy, pride, foolishness:
23 All these evil things come from within,
and defile the man.

John 13:14-15

14 If I then, your Lord and Master, have washed your feet;
ye also ought to wash one another's feet.
15 For I have given you an example,
that ye should do as I have done to you.

Romans 10:17
So then faith cometh by hearing,
and hearing by the word of God.

Examples of Like Faith

Naaman
II Kings 5:1-27

The Good Samaritan
Luke 10:30-37

Peter
Acts 10:9-16

Romans 15:4
For whatsoever things were written aforetime
were written for our learning,
that we through patience and comfort of the scriptures
might have hope.

Chapter 8

HEALTH ~~CARE~~ DARE

Mark 5:25-26
And a certain woman,
which had an issue of blood twelve years,
And had suffered many things of many physicians,
and had spent all that she had, and was nothing bettered,
but rather grew worse,

The Missionary's Experience

As the missionary makes his first hospital visit, he may wonder if he has stepped back in time. He finds himself looking at antiquated equipment, or even worse, rooms with no equipment at all. Not only does he find the technology antiquated, but the normally-provided medical supplies, such as gauze, bandages, bedding, etc., are expected to be supplied by the patient rather than the medical care providers. Then, as he finds himself sick and in need of care, he learns first-hand that the medical training and skills of those in the healthcare profession are greatly lacking. To add to his surprise, his health care provider does not even have some of the most basic sanitization resources available. He may even be given medical advice that he knows was refuted generations previous in his home country. As the missionary sits in these humble conditions, he begins to understand why so many of his colleagues have seemed to grow old early and have faced numerous health concerns without reasonable recovery. They have not been receiving health care but have rather been daring enough to allow so-called care professionals to practice on their bodies.

Biblical Examples

Dear servant of God, consider the dreadful condition of Paul as he and Silas sat in the Philippian prison. After Paul and Silas were brought before the magistrates, *"the multitude rose up together against them: and the magistrates rent off their clothes, and commanded to beat them. And when they had laid many stripes upon them, they cast them into prison"* (Acts 16:22-23). Paul and Silas had bruised bodies and open wounds, and instead of receiving sanitary medical treatment, they were thrown *"into the inner prison, and made their feet fast in the stocks"* (Acts 16:24). This place in which Paul and Silas found themselves is believed to have been one of the darkest and deepest dungeons in the city, and was most-likely filled with rodents, bugs, and the filth of other sickly imprisoned men. Yet *"at midnight Paul and Silas prayed, and sang praises unto God: and the prisoners heard them"* (Acts 16:25). They chose to look to their God rather than at the imminent dangers they had been surrounded with. They began to lift their voices to pray and sing songs to God's glory rather than lift their voices to complain about the lack of care they were receiving. Because of their God-centered focus while in the most horrible of circumstances, God heard their prayers and praises and sent an earthquake to release them from prison. Instead of rushing to find the care they so desperately needed, they stayed in those horrendously unhealthy conditions with their open wounds so that they could see the very jailer who had cast them into those unsanitary conditions be saved from death and receive the Gospel of Jesus Christ. It was then and only then that that same jailer *"washed their stripes. . . . And when he had brought them into his house, he set meat before them"* (Acts 16:33-34). Paul and Silas found themselves in the most horrible medical conditions possible, and yet they continued to glorify God with their voices and actions; and through the process they had the opportunity to make an eternal impact in the life of a man and his family.

Actual Events

As I was growing up, I had a "few" visits to local hospitals for emergencies and minor surgeries. During each of these visits, I was never concerned that they would not have all the needed supplies to care for my wounds. That level of expectation all changed within just a few months of arriving in my field of service, as I needed a minor medical procedure on one of my fingers. The doctor quickly offered to perform the operation immediately in his storefront office and proceeded to ask his assistant to go next door to a small pharmacy to purchase the needed alcohol to sterilize their instruments because they did not have any on hand. In those few minutes of waiting for the assistant to return, I considered very seriously making an excuse to leave the office. Then the doctor pulled an old machine out and began to ensure me that this cutting machine was the correct tool for the job. As I watched the physician perform the procedure, I decided I had made the wrong choice by staying, but I could no longer do anything to change the results. When I arrived home without any care or cleaning instructions, I shared with my wife my experience and clearly stated that no one else in my family would be visiting that particular doctor. Fortunately, as the years have passed and I have visited other doctors' offices and hospitals, I have been pleased to discover that not all of them operate the same way; but I have been saddened by the reality that almost none of them has an "up-to-date" level of equipment or care. These findings have been confirmed by other missionaries I have talked to, who have shared their stories of almost being killed by a doctor's extreme incorrect dosage, one missionary child who almost starved to death simply because a turntable on an x-ray machine didn't work and the hospital refused care, or the universal lack of nursing and doctor care during the birth of a child. These overwhelming realities all came to mind one Wednesday evening when I found myself rushing my nine-year-old son to the hospital with stroke-like symptoms, not knowing if they would be able to react quickly and correctly so as to prevent long-term damage. On that night, I learned what it was to not trust doctors nor complain about their lack of equipment or inability but rather to know that our God would be the only source of protection and recovery. And even though my son was provided a misdiagnosis and sent home with only the instruction to call another doctor in the morning, I praise God for the prayer of many around the world and His answer to those prayers, as he made a complete recovery without any long-term effects.

Biblical Exhortation

Dear servant of God, you must remember Who has called you to your particular field of service. You must remember Who has allowed you to face the illnesses you encounter, and you must not allow the lack of medical facilities to distract you from the love, power, and wisdom of your Heavenly Father. He is your Creator and Sustainer. He and He alone can protect you from faulty medical practices in accordance to His perfect will. You may find yourself as the woman with an issue of blood for twelve years, who *"had suffered many things of many physicians, and had spent all that she had, and was nothing bettered, but rather grew worse"* (Mark 5:26). In accordance to His perfect timing, He can heal you in a moment, as he did for her as she *"came in the press behind, and touched his garment. . . . And straightway the fountain of her blood was dried up; and she felt in her body that she was healed of that plague"* (Mark 5:26-29). Do not depend on physicians nor the level of care they may or may not provide. Do not follow the example of King Asa who *"was diseased in his feet, until his disease was exceeding great: yet in his disease he sought not to the LORD, but to the physicians . . . and died"* (II Chronicles 16:12-13). Rather, give your health and health care needs to God through prayer, and allow Him to care for you as the Great Physician, knowing that *"the prayer of faith shall save the sick, and the Lord shall raise him up"* (James 5:16).

Practical Participation

❧ **Missionary Candidate - Please prepare** yourself physically by taking care of your health and seeking medical treatment before departing for your field of service. Prepare yourself spiritually by making a purposeful practice of not depending on physicians or medical care more than in your Creator for any health concerns you encounter.

❧ **Missionary's Supporter - Please pray** for the health of your missionary. Please pray that he would enjoy good health and, when his health fails, that he would find appropriate health care for a quick and complete recovery. **Please provide** adequately for your missionary so that he can receive proper healthcare for both minor and major medical needs. Provide him the opportunity to seek appropriate health care, even if that care removes him from his field of service for a short time.

❧ **Missionary in Service - Please press on** in confidence that the finest health care in the world cannot heal your body, nor can the worst destroy it, without your loving Heavenly Father's special permission. Please press on, knowing that each health situation you face is part of God's perfect plan for your life and ministry and that He desires to use them to improve you and your ministry through them (II Corinthians 12:7-10).

Increase Your Faith

II Chronicles 16:12-13

12 And Asa in the thirty and ninth year of his reign
was diseased in his feet,
until his disease was exceeding great:
yet in his disease he sought not to the LORD,
but to the physicians.
13 And Asa slept with his fathers,
and died in the one and fortieth year of his reign.

Psalm 103:1-3

1 Bless the LORD, O my soul:
and all that is within me,
bless his holy name.
2 Bless the LORD, O my soul,
and forget not all his benefits:
3 Who forgiveth all thine iniquities;
who healeth all thy diseases;

II Corinthians 4:16-18

16 For which cause we faint not;
but though our outward man perish,
yet the inward man is renewed day by day.
17 For our light affliction, which is but for a moment,
worketh for us a far more exceeding
and eternal weight of glory;
18 While we look not at the things which are seen,
but at the things which are not seen:
for the things which are seen are temporal;
but the things which are not seen are eternal.

Philippians 2:25-27

25 Yet I supposed it necessary to send to you Epaphroditus,
my brother, and companion in labour, and fellowsoldier,
but your messenger, and he that ministered to my wants.
26 For he longed after you all, and was full of heaviness,
because that ye had heard that he had been sick.
27 For indeed he was sick nigh unto death:
but God had mercy on him;
and not on him only, but on me also,
lest I should have sorrow upon sorrow.

James 5:14-16

14 Is any sick among you?
let him call for the elders of the church;
and let them pray over him,
anointing him with oil in the name of the Lord:
15 And the prayer of faith shall save the sick,
and the Lord shall raise him up;
and if he have committed sins, they shall be forgiven him.
16 Confess your faults one to another,
and pray one for another,
that ye may be healed.
The effectual fervent prayer
of a righteous man availeth much.

III John 1:2

2 Beloved, I wish above all things
that thou mayest prosper and be in health,
even as thy soul prospereth.

Romans 10:17
So then faith cometh by hearing,
and hearing by the word of God.

Examples of Like Faith

King Hezekiah
II Kings 20:1-11

King Asa
II Chronicles 16:12-14

Woman with an Issue of Blood
Mark 5:25-34

Mary at the Birth of Jesus
Luke 2:4-7

Romans 15:4
For whatsoever things were written aforetime
were written for our learning,
that we through patience and comfort of the scriptures
might have hope.

Chapter 9

ALONE IN A CROWD

I Peter 2:11-12

Dearly beloved, I beseech you as strangers and pilgrims,
abstain from fleshly lusts, which war against the soul;
Having your conversation honest among the Gentiles:
that, whereas they speak against you as evildoers,
they may by your good works, which they shall behold,
glorify God in the day of visitation.

The Missionary's Experience

The missionary's call demands that he forsake all that is familiar to him in his homeland so that he might be an ambassador for his Lord in a foreign land, sharing the Gospel of peace with strangers (Matthew 19:27-30, Luke 5:10-11). From the moment he arrives on his field of service, he will enter a world full of crowds of people but with few, if any, familiar faces. He will find himself waiting in long lines of *people*, shuffling through large market places full of *people*, and trying to navigate traffic jams made by *people*, with none of these crowds of *people* providing any comfort for his feeling of complete loneliness. In fact, he may find himself preferring to stay at home in true solitude just to avoid the constant reminder of the loneliness he feels when he is surrounded by strangers. With each crowd, he experiences the same bitter disappointment, as he longs to encounter a comforting word or a kind smile but finds none. Even as he begins to acclimate himself to the new language and to the color of skin, eyes, and hair of those around him and starts to find some familiar faces in the local businesses he frequents, he still notices a common and disconcerting reaction from the new people he encounters. This reaction comes in the form of looks, stares, expressions of puzzlement, and even intrusive questions, as the nationals react (unconsciously or consciously) to having an obvious foreigner in their presence. Although many of these reactions are not meant to be rude or hurtful, they can still remind the missionary that he is not "at home" and produce an overwhelming sense of loneliness, even after years of being on the field. It is perhaps in these moments that he identifies best with those exotic zoo animals that have crowds of people watching them live their lives but no one with a real interest in knowing or caring for them personally. They are simply spectacles for those around them to enjoy (I Corinthians 4:9).

Biblical Examples

Dear servant of God, you are not the only one who has been different from the crowd or been alone in the midst of others. Shadrach, Meshach, and Abednego stood out, not only because of their actions, but also because of their nationality, as several Chaldeans accused them before king Nebuchadnezzar by saying, *"There are certain Jews whom thou hast set over the affairs of the province of Babylon, Shadrach, Meshach, and Abednego; these men, O king, have not regarded thee: they serve not thy gods, nor worship the golden image which thou hast set up"* (Daniel 3:12). Peter was noticed in a crowd at night for the peculiarity of his speech, just before he denied Jesus for the third time, when a group of people said, *"Surely thou also art one of them; for thy speech betrayeth thee"* (Matthew 26:73).

Even on the day of Pentecost, the disciples were identified as being different from those around them, as the question was presented by the crowd, *"Behold, are not all these which speak Galilaeans?"* (Acts 2:7). One of the clearest examples of being alone in a crowd is found in the life of Elijah as he stood in the midst of all of Israel and the 450 prophets of Baal on Mount Carmel. Although he was in the midst of his own countrymen, he stood in distinct contrast to all they believed and lived for (I Kings 18:15-37). He declared to the people of Israel *"I, even I only, remain a prophet of the LORD"* (I King 18:22). But on that day, God displayed that being alone with Him on your side is not being alone at all, as *"the fire of the LORD fell, and consumed the burnt sacrifice, and the wood, and the stones, and the dust, and licked up the water that was in the trench"* (I Kings 18:38).

Just a short time later, Elijah succumbed to the feeling of fear and loneliness, as he sought complete solitude and *"went a day's journey into the wilderness, and came and sat down under a juniper tree: and he requested for himself that he might die; and said, It is enough; now, O LORD, take away my life; for I am not better than my fathers"* (I Kings 19:4). A little while later He continued his complaint to God by saying, *"I have been very jealous for the LORD God of hosts: for the children of Israel have forsaken thy covenant, thrown down thine altars, and slain thy prophets with the sword; and I, even I only, am left; and they seek my life, to take it away"* (I Kings 19:10). Elijah perceived himself to be alone and began to wallow in self-pity. Sadly, even after God revealed Himself personally to Elijah, he continued to believe the same human fallacy, as he said once again, *"I have been very jealous for the LORD God of hosts: because the children of Israel have forsaken thy covenant, thrown down thine altars, and slain thy prophets with the sword; and I, even I only, am left; and they seek my life, to take it away"* (I Kings 19:14). God's response was clear. Elijah was not alone, for he had *"seven thousand in Israel, all the knees which have not bowed unto Baal, and every mouth which hath not kissed him"* (I Kings 19:18).

Although Elijah did not have these seven thousand physically by his side at that very moment, he did have seven thousand individuals who were just like him and who were serving the same God. In God's kindness to Elijah's need for companionship, He sent him to find Elisha, who *"went after Elijah, and ministered unto him"* until the end of his life (I Kings 19:21). God recognized Elijah's need for human companionship and provided a companion in accordance with His perfect timing. And so it is for missionaries. Even though our ministries take us to distant lands, where no companions are close at hand, we must never forget that we are not alone. First, because God is on our side. Second, because there are others serving the same God. And third, because, in God's perfect timing, He will provide us the human companionship we need.

Actual Events

My arrival on my field of service was very different from what I had planned. I had expected that the Lord would use me in an area of the country where I already knew several other missionaries and could enjoy their fellowship from the beginning. However, while I was in language school, I was informed by my future co-workers that they were not going to be ministering in that area any longer. They were going to take a church about an hour away. So, as I sought the Lord's direction for housing and establishing our new lives and ministry, I believed it was best to live in the town in which the church was located. This placed us a great distance from fellow missionaries and even from our co-workers, who still owned their home an hour and fifteen minutes away. As well, I lived in an area of the country with much less English influence and where a good number of the people do not like outsiders. As I traveled around town, I was quickly noticed and even resisted by some. Thankfully, the Lord gave me kind neighbors, who took the time to get to know me. But on many occasions, I hesitated to leave the "safe haven" of our home to enter the center stage of the crowd.

Over time, I became accustomed to the puzzled expressions or even comments and questions about my light skin, blue eyes, and light brown hair. I grew to enjoy the curious stares of some of the children who had never seen such features and kindly responded to the equally curious questions from adults who were anxious to know where I was from and why I was living in their town. Being accustomed to being different does not always mean being comfortable with the reality. There is a sense of discomfort in knowing that your actions, words, etc., are easily noticed by all, even when you are not aware of it. On one specific occasion, my deacon shared with me that he was talking to an acquaintance about our church. The acquaintance quickly responded, "I know your church, your pastor is the short, American man." Wow, this man knew who I was without me knowing anything about him or ever meeting him personally. To this day, I have no idea what that man knows about me or what I may or may not have done to him, but because I am different, he will never forget me and will probably never stop watching me from a distance.

Even after years of being on the field, I found myself being stared at by a young girl while standing in line at the store, and on another occasion an elderly lady specifically asked me if I was American after noticing my children and the color of our hair and eyes but that we could speak the local language. In moments like these, we often find ourselves wrestling with the original sense of loneliness we felt when we first arrived. Oh, how I long to simply "fit in." But then God kindly reminds me that if we are spiritual *"strangers and pilgrims"* on this earth, I should not feel so devastated by being a physical stranger and pilgrim as well (I Peter 2:11).

Biblical Exhortation

Dear servant of God, do not allow being a spectacle to overwhelm you. Rather recognize that God created you specifically the way you are so that you can have a specific impact in the lives of those to whom He has sent you (Jeremiah 1:4-8). Accept the responsibility and opportunity that comes from being "different" from those around you. Recognize that, because you are different, you are being watched. Therefore, live every moment of your life as a good *"ambassador for Christ"* (II Corinthians 5:20). Remember that questions caused by your physical difference will often open the door of opportunity for you to fulfill your calling of kindly sharing God's love and message of salvation.

Practical Participation

✎ **Missionary Candidate - Please prepare** yourself for human loneliness by developing a deep and meaningful relationship with your Lord, Who will be with you throughout your entire ministry. Prepare yourself by accepting opportunities to minister to new people and in new places so that you might begin to experience the joy of serving and building new relationships with strangers.

✎ **Missionary's Supporter - Please pray** for your missionary as he faces the crowds on a daily basis. Please pray that God would quickly provide kind nationals or other like-minded missionaries so that he is able to begin to once again hear welcoming words and see kind faces in his new world and that he might quickly feel at "home" with those around him. **Please provide** your missionary with kind words of encouragement (spoken and written), which reassure him of your dedication to the same cause of Christ, even though there is a great physical distance between you.

✎ **Missionary in Service - Please press on** knowing that, while you may be alone physically, Jesus Christ has promised to be with you at all times (Matthew 28:18-20). Please press on with the assurance that God will provide others to join you in His perfect timing. Do not become distracted from your God-given task of reaching the lost simply because you do not know them yet. Rather, look forward to getting to know each new person you encounter, with the anticipation that they could become a brother or sister in Christ and a fellow companion in the labor of God's ministry.

Increase Your Faith

Jeremiah 1:4-10

4 Then the word of the LORD came unto me, saying,
5 Before I formed thee in the belly I knew thee;
and before thou camest forth out of the womb
I sanctified thee,
and I ordained thee a prophet unto the nations.
6 Then said I, Ah, Lord GOD! behold, I cannot speak:
for I am a child.
7 But the LORD said unto me, Say not, I am a child:
for thou shalt go to all that I shall send thee,
and whatsoever I command thee thou shalt speak.
8 Be not afraid of their faces:
for I am with thee to deliver thee, saith the LORD.
9 Then the LORD put forth his hand, and touched my mouth.
And the LORD said unto me,
Behold, I have put my words in thy mouth.
10 See, I have this day set thee over the nation
and over the kingdoms,
to root out, and to pull down, and to destroy,
and to throw down,
to build, and to plant.

Matthew 28:18-20

18 And Jesus came and spake unto them, saying,
All power is given unto me in heaven and in earth.
19 Go ye therefore, and teach all nations,
baptizing them in the name of the Father,
and of the Son, and of the Holy Ghost:
20 Teaching them to observe all things
whatsoever I have commanded you:
and, lo, I am with you alway,
even unto the end of the world.
Amen.

Mark 10:29-30

29 And Jesus answered and said, Verily I say unto you,
There is no man that hath left house,
or brethren, or sisters, or father, or mother,
or wife, or children, or lands, for my sake, and the gospel's,
30 But he shall receive an hundredfold now in this time,
houses, and brethren, and sisters,
and mothers, and children, and lands,
with persecutions;
and in the world to come eternal life.

Romans 15:20-21

20 Yea, so have I strived to preach the gospel,
not where Christ was named,
lest I should build upon another man's foundation:
21 But as it is written,
To whom he was not spoken of, they shall see:
and they that have not heard shall understand.

II Timothy 4:16-18

16 At my first answer no man stood with me,
but all men forsook me:
I pray God that it may not be laid to their charge.
17 Notwithstanding the Lord stood with me,
and strengthened me;
that by me the preaching might be fully known,
and that all the Gentiles might hear:
and I was delivered out of the mouth of the lion.
18 And the Lord shall deliver me from every evil work,
and will preserve me unto his heavenly kingdom:
to whom be glory for ever and ever. Amen.

Hebrews 11:13

*13 These all died in faith,
not having received the promises,
but having seen them afar off,
and were persuaded of them, and embraced them,
and confessed that they were
strangers and pilgrims on the earth.*

Romans 10:17
So then faith cometh by hearing,
and hearing by the word of God.

Examples of Like Faith

Abraham
Genesis 23:1-6

Paul
Acts 17:15-34

Romans 15:4
For whatsoever things were written aforetime
were written for our learning,
that we through patience and comfort of the scriptures
might have hope.

Chapter 10

SEEING BEYOND THE FOG

Colossians 3:2
*Set your affection on things above,
not on things on the earth.*

The Missionary's Experience

While the missionary is sharing his plans for ministry with other believers and preparing himself to leave his homeland, he finds himself living a life of "faith": a life that is completely focused on *"things hoped for"* but *"not seen"* as of yet (Hebrews 11:1). He has dedicated his time, prayer, and energy to live for the promises of Scripture, and, as he leaves all he knows and cares for behind, he steps by faith into an unknown world with only one assurance: Jesus's promise of *"lo, I am with you alway, even unto the end of the world. Amen"* (Matthew 28:20). He is making spiritual decisions that many others never make, all with the desire to fulfill God's command to *"set your affection on things above, not on things on the earth"* (Colossians 3:2). However, when he arrives in his new land, where everything around him is strange, he finds himself experiencing a sensory overload and a nervous panic due to the constant bombardment of his physical environment. His sense of touch is distracted by the new climate. His sense of taste is distracted by the new flavors and textures of the food. His sense of smell is distracted by uncleanliness. His sense of hearing is distracted by the sounds of the new language and surroundings. And his sense of sight is distracted by sights totally unfamiliar and shocking to him. With each new event, he finds himself so distracted by his physical world that he cannot seem to see beyond the fog of the physical world to concentrate on the spiritual reason he had come to this new world. Although his heart longs to feel the security and confidence he had while in his homeland, spending hours reading God's Word, praying, and talking to fellow believers, he struggles to be able to read one simple verse without being distracted by a new insect crossing his path, the sound of traffic, or the smell of the trash baking in the heat of the sun. In these days, weeks, and months, the missionary will greatly question his faith. He will long for, but doubt he will ever once again know, the quiet peace of allowing the world around him to fade into the distance so that he might spend a few moments enjoying the calming effect of *"looking for that blessed hope, and the glorious appearing of the great God and our Saviour Jesus Christ"* (Titus 2:13).

Biblical Examples

Dear servant of God, Peter experienced the same overwhelming pressure you are facing. He, unlike any of the other disciples, was willing to trust Jesus Christ and follow him into the unknown, with the hope of accomplishing the unimaginable. As Jesus came walking to the disciples on the water in the midst of the storm, Peter said, *"Lord, if it be thou, bid me come unto thee on the water"* (Matthew 14:28). And when Jesus said, *"Come,"* Peter came *"down out of the ship, he walked on the water, to go to Jesus"* (Matthew 14:29). Peter had faith to trust Jesus's call upon his life to do something no other man had ever done. He was a man of action as he quickly left the safety of his boat and stepped onto the water. He had accomplished what the other eleven disciples did not dare attempt. *"But when he saw the wind boisterous, he was afraid"* (Matthew 14:30). Peter was walking in obedience to his Lord. He was experiencing God's protection and blessing. But his physical senses were overwhelmed by the physical realities around him so that his spiritual sense of faith began to fail. There was no doubt that what was distracting Peter was physically real. The winds, waves, and the sounds around him were not imagined. But they should not have been his focus. "*And beginning to sink, he cried, saying, Lord, save me*" (Matthew 14:30). As Peter became distracted by his physical circumstances, those circumstance began to affect him, and he began to sink into his physical problems rather than living above them. But as he once again turned his attention to his Lord and found his faith renewed, his surrounding circumstances faded away, as "*immediately Jesus stretched forth his hand, and caught him, and said unto him, O thou of little faith, wherefore didst thou doubt*" (Matthew 14:31)?

Elisha's servant also experienced extreme fear, when he could not see beyond the physical world around him. The king of Syria had sent "*horses, and chariots, and a great host: and they came by night, and compassed the city about*" where Elisha and his servant were living (II Kings 6:14). When Elisha's servant woke up in the morning and saw the "*host compassed the city both with horses and chariots,*" he said, "*Alas, my master! how shall we do*" (II Kings 6:15). Elisha's answer was simple: "*Fear not: for they that be with us are more than they that be with them*" (II Kings 6:16). That answer must have been very confusing for the servant as he saw the "*great host*" of soldiers all around him and Elisha as they stood all alone. The physical world portrayed something very different than what Elisha saw. So "*Elisha prayed, and said, LORD, I pray thee, open his eyes, that he may see. And the LORD opened the eyes of the young man; and he saw: and, behold, the mountain was full of horses and chariots of fire round about Elisha*" (II Kings 6:17).

Actual Events

The first months in my field of service were filled with distractions. Daily, moment by moment, the physical world with its newness and difficulties constantly cried for my attention. As I sought to take time alone with my God on a walk, I was distracted by the newness of the style of homes. As I sought to read my Bible, the noise of the loudspeaker truck blaring its announcements prevented my concentration. About the time I thought I might have a few moments free from dealing with physical issues of the day, I would receive a phone call or a neighbor would need some help. These pressures mounted until, one day, I said in frustration to my wife, "I thought I was spiritually sound in my faith, that my attention and action of serving God was proof of my spiritual desire and focus. But now I think I must be the most carnal missionary to ever live. I simply cannot get the newness, needs, and distractions of this physical world out of my mind so that I can concentrate on my Lord and the spiritual ministry He has entrusted to me." To aid me in my concentration, I took refuge in a small four-by-five-foot closet in our home and made it my office (no windows), found a headset so that I could listen to music to finally drown out my new world, and sought some consistency and familiarity in my spiritual life and studies. Over time, and as the strangeness of my surroundings became the norm for my new life, my sensory overload and the sense of panic subsided. I was able to once again live with the physical world around me, while regularly looking past those circumstances to my Lord and Savior Jesus Christ, to follow God's command to "*Be still, and know that I am God*" (Psalm 46:10).

Biblical Exhortation

Dear servant of God, the physical world will constantly fight to keep your attention. The difficulties you have in being able to distinguish between what is physically real and what is spiritually real are no different than at other times in your life; they are simply more intense. God has created you with the ability to observe your surroundings through your five senses for your protection and enjoyment, but Satan will attempt to change all of that to bring about your downfall. As you find yourself struggling to see beyond the fog of this physical world, make a more dedicated effort to call to the Lord in prayer and ask Him to calm your heart and clear your confusion so that "*the eyes of your understanding being enlightened; that ye may know what is the hope of his calling, and what the riches of the glory of his inheritance in the saints, and what is the exceeding greatness of his power to us-ward who believe, according to the working of his mighty power*" (Ephesians 1:18-19). Continually remember that "*the just shall live by faith: but if any man draw back, my soul shall have no pleasure in him*"

(Hebrews 10:38). Do not allow the things around you to distract you from God but rather to push you closer to God. Allow each new sight, sound, texture, smell, and taste to remind you of the greatness of God's creation and His unmeasured love to send His Son to live in the same conditions you are experiencing, to save you and those around you from their sins. Remember that *"our light affliction, which is but for a moment, worketh for us a far more exceeding and eternal weight of glory; while we look not at the things which are seen, but at the things which are not seen: for the things which are seen are temporal; but the things which are not seen are eternal"* (II Corinthians 4:17-18). And purposefully *"seek ye first the kingdom of God, and his righteousness"* and allow God to take care of your physical surroundings (Matthew 6:33).

Practical Participation

✎ **Missionary Candidate - Please prepare** your spiritual life for the distractions of the physical world. Establish habits of daily removing yourself from your busy schedule and noisy world to enjoy fellowship with God. Specifically memorize passages of Scripture that will help you in times of anxiety by drawing your attention back to the greatness of God.

✎ **Missionary's Supporter - Please pray** for your missionary as he is confronted on a daily, moment-by-moment basis with new and frightening circumstances. Pray that he will find a place of quiet rest from the physical world where he can concentrate and enjoy his personal relationship with his Lord and Savior. **Please provide** him with small reminders of God's constant care through cards of encouragement, recorded sermons, etc., which he can use to fill his heart and life with the calming reminders of his Savior while removing the clamor of his physical world.

✎ **Missionary in Service - Please press on** by understanding the reality of the physical world around you as well as your need to keep your eyes on your Savior in order to save you from that reality. Press on by regularly making time to be "still" and know more of who God is so that you can adequately do more for Him when it is time for you to be busy. Press on by calling out to God and asking Him to renew your faith when you are distracted from Him and begin to sink in the problems of the physical world around you. Press on by *"looking unto Jesus the author and finisher of our faith; who for the joy that was set before him endured the cross, despising the shame, and is set down at the right hand of the throne of God. For consider him that endured such contradiction of sinners against himself, lest ye be wearied and faint in your minds."* (Hebrews 12:2-3).

Increase Your Faith

Psalm 42:5, 7-8

5 *Why art thou cast down, O my soul?*
and why art thou disquieted in me?
hope thou in God:
for I shall yet praise him
for the help of his countenance.
7 *Deep calleth unto deep at the noise of thy waterspouts:*
all thy waves and thy billows are gone over me.
8 *Yet the LORD will command his lovingkindness*
in the daytime,
and in the night his song shall be with me,
and my prayer unto the God of my life.

Psalm 46:10-11

10 *Be still, and know that I am God:*
I will be exalted among the heathen,
I will be exalted in the earth.
11 *The LORD of hosts is with us;*
the God of Jacob is our refuge. Selah.

Psalm 61:1-4

1 *Hear my cry, O God; attend unto my prayer.*
2 *From the end of the earth will I cry unto thee,*
when my heart is overwhelmed:
lead me to the rock that is higher than I.
3 *For thou hast been a shelter for me,*
and a strong tower from the enemy.
4 *I will abide in thy tabernacle for ever:*
I will trust in the covert of thy wings. Selah.

II Corinthians 4:16-18

16 For which cause we faint not;
but though our outward man perish,
yet the inward man is renewed day by day.
17 For our light affliction, which is but for a moment,
worketh for us a far more exceeding
and eternal weight of glory;
18 While we look not at the things which are seen,
but at the things which are not seen:
for the things which are seen are temporal;
but the things which are not seen are eternal.

II Corinthians 5:7

7 (For we walk by faith, not by sight:)

Hebrews 11:1, 6

1 Now faith is the substance of things hoped for,
the evidence of things not seen.
6 But without faith it is impossible to please him:
for he that cometh to God must believe that he is,
and that he is a rewarder of them that diligently seek him.

Hebrews 12:1-3

*1 Wherefore seeing we also are compassed about
with so great a cloud of witnesses,
let us lay aside every weight,
and the sin which doth so easily beset us,
and let us run with patience the race that is set before us,
2 Looking unto Jesus the author and finisher of our faith;
who for the joy that was set before him endured the cross,
despising the shame,
and is set down at the right hand of the throne of God.
3 For consider him that endured
such contradiction of sinners against himself,
lest ye be wearied and faint in your minds.*

Romans 10:17
So then faith cometh by hearing,
and hearing by the word of God.

Examples of Like Faith

Shadrach, Meshach, and Abednego
Daniel 3:20-26

Daniel
Daniel 6:16-23

Jesus
Matthew 14:22-23
Mark 35-41

Paul and Silas
Acts 16:23-26

Romans 15:4
For whatsoever things were written aforetime
were written for our learning,
that we through patience and comfort of the scriptures
might have hope.

Chapter 11

BEARING THE BURDEN ALONE

II Corinthians 2:12-13
Furthermore, when I came to Troas to preach Christ's gospel,
and a door was opened unto me of the Lord,
I had no rest in my spirit, because I found not Titus my brother:
but taking my leave of them, I went from thence into Macedonia.

The Missionary's Experience

The missionary serving on the foreign field will almost definitely face the overwhelming responsibility of caring for the Lord's work without any other full-time co-laborers or mature believers to work by his side. During these times, whether they be for months or years, he will most likely find himself both physically and spiritually exhausted. The constant pressure of the weekly preaching and teaching schedule is often magnified as he prepares his studies in a second language. As well, the tedious counseling situations he encounters because of the destroyed lives lived in a godless society will often require much time and effort both in prayer and study while he seeks to present sound, Bible- based advice joined with adequate time for personal interaction and accountability required by the one being counseled. Amidst each of these spiritual burdens, he will feel the loss of not having a "multitude of counselors" so that he can find "*safety*" and find his "*purposes*" or plans "*established*" (Proverbs 11:14, 15:22). And yet, he will maintain the responsibility of organizing, preparing, and executing all of the normal and special ministries of the church, all while keeping the building cleaned and grounds nicely groomed. In the end, he will begin to ask God for twenty-eight hours in his day and the physical stamina to accomplish each task with little, or no, sleep. His job is not finished by just maintaining the ministry; he must constantly seek and prepare for future ministry opportunities to extend the impact of the Gospel. And he will often feel as though he is working with one hand tied behind his back as he has no one to go with him on visitation and discipleship. To add to the weight of the burden, it is also during these exhausting ministry occasions that Satan will plan and execute specific attacks of temptation so as destroy him while he is tired and weak. Satan seeks to distract the missionary from his dependence on his all-sufficient God, Who never fails to provide the means needed to accomplish His commandments.

Biblical Examples

Dear servant of God, the Apostle Paul always sought companions in ministry. But, on occasion, he, too, found himself lacking the physical presence of co-laborers. In Acts 17:15, when he found himself alone in Athens, he sent "*a commandment unto Silas and Timotheus for to come to him with all speed.*" Paul longed for assistance and fellowship in his ministry, and so he commanded his co-laborers to come to him as fast as possible. He recognized the importance of team missions and the limitations of ministering alone. However, he did not forsake his calling to proclaim the Gospel just because he was without co-laborers. Instead, "*while Paul waited for them at Athens, his spirit was stirred in him, when he saw the city wholly given to idolatry. Therefore disputed he in the synagogue with the Jews, and with the devout persons, and in the market daily with them that met with him.*" Paul continued to minister to the best of his ability even though he was alone. This faithful ministering, although limited, produced a great opportunity for Paul to present the truth about the "*UNKNOWN GOD*" on Mars' hill (Acts 17:22-31). While no church is said to have been started on that day, Paul's ministry did have an eternal impact, as "*certain men clave unto him, and believed: among the which was Dionysius the Areopagite, and a woman named Damaris, and others with them*" (Acts 17:34).

A short time later, Paul found himself once again seeking companionship from his co-laborer. II Corinthians 2:12-13 says, *"Furthermore, when I came to Troas to preach Christ's gospel, and a door was opened unto me of the Lord, I had no rest in my spirit, because I found not Titus my brother: but taking my leave of them, I went from thence into Macedonia."* Paul, even with a God-given opportunity to minister, lacked the peace that he desired, because he did not have Titus's fellowship. Paul continues to share his burden of ministering alone by saying, *"For, when we were come into Macedonia, our flesh had no rest, but we were troubled on every side; without were fightings, within were fears"* (II Corinthians 7:5). Paul's ministry was not easy, due to outward attacks and inward fears, and these pressures added to his desire for a familiar face and helping hand. So, in II Corinthians 7:6, Paul expresses his personal relief, as he was once again joined by his co-laborer, Titus. He says, *"Nevertheless God, that comforteth those that are cast down, comforted us by the coming of Titus."*

Paul's example reveals the natural desire for, and the importance of, having assistance in the ministry. But it also displays that God, on occasion, expects his ministers to be faithful when they are working alone. They must not give in to the frustration and exhaustion, as Moses did when he said, *"Wherefore hast thou afflicted thy servant? and wherefore have I not found favour in thy sight, that thou layest the burden of all this people upon me? . . . I am not able to bear all this people alone, because it is too heavy for me. And if thou deal thus with me, kill me, I pray thee"* (Numbers 11:11-15). But rather they must patiently await God's wise counsel and provision of other spiritual leaders so that *"they shall bear the burden of the people with thee [them], that thou [they] bear it not thyself [themselves] alone"* (Numbers 11:16-18).

Actual Events

I am very thankful that God provided co-laborers in ministry for my first term on the field. However, during this first term, there were several occasions in which I was left alone on the field so that my co-laborers could take their furloughs. On these occasions, the pressure of ministry was high, and the expectations that nothing would be missed, even though part of the team was missing, was a little overwhelming. But

God, by His wisdom, guided me to fulfill every responsibility adequately, and through His gracious strength, allowed me to continue to make an impact in the lives around me. As my first term came to an end and I took my furlough, I knew that the health and age of our co-workers would most likely mean my returning to bear the full burden of the ministry alone. This anticipation was both exciting and daunting. I very quickly began to ask God to provide some helpers who could help bear part of the burden. And that was exactly what God did. He sent me a retired couple for a year and half, who, although they could not minister **publicly** in spiritual things, sacrificed their time and energy to minister in many physical ways, which allowed me the time needed to minister in the spiritual matters. As well, their kind friendship and consistent prayers continued to motivate me to move forward in the work of the Lord even when I felt limited due to the lack of laborers. However, the Lord's timing for this couple's departure came suddenly, as they had a disappointing and unexpected need to return home. After their departure, I recall thinking to myself, "What will I do now? There is no way that I can accomplish the spiritual ministry while caring for the physical needs of the church property." I, like Paul, sensed the bitter sorrow of loneliness as I missed the consistent kindness and encouragement from these believers. And to make matters worse, I found myself in a difficult period of ministry in which "*our flesh had no rest, but we were troubled on every side; without were fightings, within were fears*" (II Corinthians 7:5). So, I once again began to anxiously wait on the Lord to fill the gap. Little did I know that the "*God, that comforteth those that are cast down, comforted [would comfort] us by the coming of*" fellow believers who would visit and minister to us (II Corinthians 7:6).

Biblical Exhortation

Dear servant of God, do not quit ministering just because you lack assistance. Be reasonable in your limitations as you long for and pray earnestly about your need for co-laborers in ministry. And then stay faithful in the tasks that you have the ability to accomplish, while asking God to graciously fill in the gaps where you are lacking. God knows that you are but dust.

Practical Participation

✎ **Missionary Candidate - Please prepare** yourself well for all aspects of ministry so that you are capable of ministering without co-laborers by your side. Prepare yourself by wisely asking counsel of those presently around you but by not relying on them alone to make your spiritual decisions and future plans. Be sure to regularly turn to God's Word for wisdom and pray to God for strength and guidance in every step of your daily life.

✎ **Missionary's Supporter - Please pray** for your missionary as he ministers alone. Please pray that God will provide him with special wisdom, as he must make constant decisions without adequate counsel. Please also pray that God will provide extra strength as he goes about maintaining both the spiritual and physical needs of the ministry without adequate assistance. **Please provide** refreshing opportunities for fellowship and rest when your missionary is on furlough so that he can recuperate from his lonely and exhausting work on the field. Provide opportunities for your missionary to expand his ministry training when he finds an area in which he feels he has an inadequate background. Provide your missionary with helping hands through individual as well as small group mission trips in order to help him accomplish specific spiritual and physical goals in the ministry.

✎ **Missionary in Service - Please press on** with a complete dependence upon God and His Word to guide you as you make realistic ministry plans and seek to accomplish those plans in God's might. Please press on in the strength God has provided and do not allow the physical exhaustion to take away from the spiritual contentment of knowing you are accomplishing a special calling as God's ambassador to a people who will have no message of peace if you fail (evidenced by no one else being where you are to share the message).

Increase Your Faith

Isaiah 14:9-10

9 Thou whom I have taken from the ends of the earth,
and called thee from the chief men thereof,
and said unto thee, Thou art my servant;
I have chosen thee, and not cast thee away.
10 Fear thou not; for I am with thee:
be not dismayed; for I am thy God:
I will strengthen thee;
yea, I will help thee;
yea, I will uphold thee
with the right hand of my righteousness.

Isaiah 40:27-31

27 Why sayest thou, O Jacob, and speakest, O Israel,
My way is hid from the LORD,
And my judgment is passed over from my God?
28 Hast thou not known? hast thou not heard,
That the everlasting God, the LORD,
The Creator of the ends of the earth,
Fainteth not, neither is weary?
There is no searching of his understanding.
29 He giveth power to the faint;
And to them that have no might he increaseth strength.
30 Even the youths shall faint and be weary,
And the young men shall utterly fall:
31 But they that wait upon the LORD
shall renew their strength;
They shall mount up with wings as eagles;
They shall run, and not be weary;
And they shall walk, and not faint.

II Corinthians 4:1-5

1 Therefore seeing we have this ministry,
as we have received mercy, we faint not;
2 But have renounced the hidden things of dishonesty,
not walking in craftiness,
nor handling the word of God deceitfully;
but by manifestation of the truth
commending ourselves to every man's conscience
in the sight of God.
3 But if our gospel be hid, it is hid to them that are lost:
4 In whom the god of this world
hath blinded the minds of them which believe not,
lest the light of the glorious gospel of Christ,
who is the image of God,
should shine unto them.
5 For we preach not ourselves, but Christ Jesus the Lord;
and ourselves your servants for Jesus' sake.

Galatians 6:9

9 And let us not be weary in well doing:
for in due season we shall reap, if we faint not.

Hebrews 13:5-6

5 Let your conversation be without covetousness;
and be content with such things as ye have:
for he hath said, I will never leave thee, nor forsake thee.
6 So that we may boldly say, The Lord is my helper,
and I will not fear what man shall do unto me.

Romans 10:17
So then faith cometh by hearing,
and hearing by the word of God.

Examples of Like Faith

Moses
Numbers 11:10-17

David
I Samuel 17:19-30

Samson
Judges 16:23-31

Romans 15:4
For whatsoever things were written aforetime
were written for our learning,
that we through patience and comfort of the scriptures
might have hope.

Chapter 12

CONFLICTS IN CO-LABORING

Ecclesiastes 4:9
Two are better than one;
because they have a good reward for their labour.

The Missionary's Experience

The missionary who is preparing himself for service on the foreign field may be expected to work alongside a veteran missionary for at least the first year or two. But if he expresses his desire to work with co-workers indefinitely, he will most-likely find himself receiving disconcerted looks and counsel to the contrary. Sadly, most of the warnings will be based on the horrifying stories of past missionaries who simply could not get along. He may begin to believe that Paul's pattern of ministering with others to be simply impractical in his day. All of this false advertisement against the Biblical pattern of ministry can very quickly set the stage for his failure as a co-laborer before he even starts. Sadly, what he may not realize is that although the "headlines" have been written about the failures in such a style of ministry, many more stories could be written about humble and faithful men and women who have enjoyed the privilege of working together with great success. He may not even realize that almost all of the famous missionaries, whose names he had heard and read about, such as Hudson Taylor, William Cary, Jim Elliot, Adoniram Judson, etc., all enjoyed the privilege of companions in ministry. Many of these and others like them would have never accomplished such great ministries for the Lord, nor be known today, if they had not had others who co-labored with them.

With all of the warnings received, rather than spiritual encouragement, the young missionary's first impression of the veteran servant of God may have been tainted by thoughts of skepticism and self-protection from the very ones he should respect and learn from before they ever meet. In like fashion, because of the same ill-informed counsel and warnings given to the veteran missionary, he may also begin his new relationship with the young missionary with reluctance rather than anticipation. In the initial weeks and months, while the young missionary starts to acclimate himself to his new world, the two missionaries will have many opportunities to communicate either their mutual respect and care or disrespect and disregard for each other through their words and actions. As well, this crucial time will provide opportunities for their expectations of each other to be realized or dashed. With each dashed expectation, each one will be given the important opportunity to kindly forgive and learn or become embittered and resentful.

When a new missionary arrives on his field of service, he will most likely discover that the veteran missionary of many years is just as human as any other man or woman. He may discover that he, too, faces sickness and discouragements, fails other people's expectations, and even on some occasions commits sins. This discovery can be extremely devastating, as the young missionary had dreamed of serving alongside the "perfect" co-worker and finding co-laboring to be natural and without effort. The young missionary must quickly readjust his level of expectations, and in many cases, so must the veteran missionary. These readjustments are not easily made, as they are often revealed through differences and disagreements, which must be handled with graciousness and forgiveness.

Biblical Examples

Dear servant of God, the Scripture is clear: *"Two are better than one; because they have a good reward for their labour"* (Ecclesiastes 4:9). Jesus Christ often performed His ministry with

His team of twelve disciples. As He was ministering throughout the villages, *"He called unto him the twelve, and began to send them forth by two and two;"* and later in his ministry he sent the seventy disciples *"two and two before his face into every city and place, whither he himself would come"* (Mark 6:7, Luke 10:1). And as He commanded his disciples to find him a colt for His triumphal entry into Jerusalem, *"he sent two of his disciples"* (Luke 19:29). God approved this same pattern of co-laboring as he initiated Paul's missionary ministry—*"the Holy Ghost said, Separate me Barnabas and Saul for the work whereunto I have called them . . . and they had also John to their minister."* (Acts 13:2, 5).

Unfortunately, Jesus and Paul faced the disappointment of desertion from one of their co-laborers. Judas Iscariot deserted and betrayed Jesus for a little silver (Mathew 26:14-16), and John Mark deserted Paul because of the pressure and attacks of the ministry (Acts 13:13). Although those who departed caused great sorrow, neither Jesus nor Paul saw any reason to give up or deny others who desired to co-labor with them. Paul faced the disappointment of friction with one of his co-laborers, as he and Barnabas disagreed about John Mark traveling with them on their second missionary journey (Acts 15:36-40). *"And the contention was so sharp between them, that they departed asunder one from the other: and so Barnabas took Mark, and sailed unto Cyprus; And Paul chose Silas, and departed, being recommended by the brethren unto the grace of God"* (Acts 15:39-40). Although Paul's first co-laboring experience did not end pleasantly with John Mark, he did later request Timothy to *"take Mark, and bring him with thee: for he is profitable to me for the ministry"* (II Timothy 4:11). He also immediately replaced Barnabas with Silas and continued the co-laboring style of ministry that he followed until the end of his life.

On one occasion, Paul found himself alone in Athens, patiently awaiting his co-laborers' arrival, and because *"his spirit was stirred in him, when he saw the city wholly given to idolatry,"* he was moved to minister without his normal companions. This event ended in lives being changed and souls being saved, but his normal pattern of planting a church is never mentioned. This example serves as a reminder of the importance to continue in ministry as God provides opportunity, even when co-laborers are lacking, and to always look for the blessing of working alongside another servant of God for the "*good reward*" of the labor (Ecclesiastes 4:9). The Apostle Paul clearly desired companionship in ministry, and he felt the discouragement of loneliness when he did not have it. He shared with the church at Corinth that "*when I [he] came to Troas to preach Christ's gospel, and a door was opened unto me of the Lord, I [he] had no rest in my [his] spirit, because I [he] found not Titus my brother*" (II Corinthians 2:12-13). Paul, the great warrior for the Gospel of Christ, found himself without "*rest*" because he missed his co-laborer, Titus. So He continued to travel to Macedonia to find Titus, even though he had a great opportunity for ministry in Troas. After arriving in Macedonia and being joined by Titus, Paul said, "*our flesh had no rest, but we were troubled on every side; without were fightings, within were fears. Nevertheless God, that comforteth those that are cast down, comforted us by the coming of Titus*" (II Corinthians 7:5-6). Co-laborers can cause difficulties through desertion and disagreement, but if team members will dedicate themselves to a God-centered unity, they will provide needed comfort and counsel for one another. "*Two are better than one; because they have a good reward for their labour. For if they fall, the one will lift up his fellow: but woe to him that is alone when he falleth; for he hath not another to help him up. Again, if two lie together, then they have heat: but how can one be warm alone? And if one prevail against him, two shall withstand him; and a threefold cord is not quickly broken*" (Ecclesiastes 4:9-12).

Actual Events

As I remember my privileged opportunities to co-labor with fellow men and women of God in the ministry, both in my homeland and my mission field, I must honestly say that there have been great blessings and great disappointments. I am sure that those who worked with me could say the same, no matter how hard I may have attempted to eliminate any cause for disappointment. Perhaps those disappointing moments while co-laboring in my homeland were part of God's preparation for those I would face while living in a strange and difficult place without the helpfulness and closeness I had hoped for from my missionary co-laborers. Regardless of the specific details of my disappointment, the reality of desertion in time of need and disagreement in ministry philosophy and practice have taken their toll. At times, I have had to make sure I was not influenced by the disappointing counsel mentioned earlier. I have had to search the Scriptures to re-commit myself to the Biblical pattern of co-laboring and find where I had failed so that I could make the proper corrections for future opportunities. As God has provided new co-laborers, I have had to regularly ask God for wisdom so as to make our working and personal relationship the best possible. I have had to ensure that my expectations of others are realistic while always seeking to *"very gladly spend and be spent for"* them (II Corinthians 12:15). I have needed to remember the humble example of our Lord as He washed His disciples' feet and said, *"Know ye what I have done to you? Ye call me Master and Lord: and ye say well; for so I am. If I then, your Lord and Master, have washed your feet; ye also ought to wash one another's feet. For I have given you an example, that ye should do as I have done to you"* (John 13:12-15).

Biblical Exhortation

Dear servant of God, are you committed to follow God's pattern for co-laboring? Have you been asking God to provide you with the correct teammates for the work of the ministry? When God has provided you with that privileged opportunity to co-labor with brothers and sisters in Christ, have you fulfilled your part? Have you committed yourself to serve as Christ served? If you have not yet considered co-laboring as a great privilege and Biblical pattern, will you begin to do so now? The work of the Lord is too great for us to go about fighting and feuding over prideful differences. We must work together in accordance with God's Word. For *"two are better than one; because they have a good reward for their labour. For if they fall, the one will lift up his fellow: but woe to him that is alone when he falleth; for he hath not another to help him up. Again, if two lie together, then they have heat: but how can one be warm alone? And if one prevail against him, two shall withstand him;*

and a threefold cord is not quickly broken" (Ecclesiastes 4:9-12). Commit today to allow God to be the first part, your co-labor the second part, and yourself the third part of the "*threefold cord*" which "*is not quickly broken*" (Ecclesiastes 4:12).

Practical Participation

🖎 **Missionary Candidate - Please prepare** yourself by working to maintain a Biblically humble relationship with others as you gain ministry training and experience. Prepare yourself by studying and understanding the proper roles of leadership and their subordinates. Prepare yourself by diligently praying for God to send you the correct co-laborers and to protect you and them from any unresolvable conflicts.

🖎 **Missionary's Supporter - Please pray** that the relationships your missionary establishes on the mission field would be long lasting for the glory of God and the advancement of His Gospel. Please pray that team members would adequately fulfill their responsibilities and lovingly edify each other in times of need. **Please provide** your missionary with Biblically-based counsel if relationship differences arise. And provide your missionary the same grace you would desire when conflicts do arise and ministry changes.

🖎 **Missionary in Service - Please press on** in your ministry relationships with the knowledge that God has established them for your good and His glory. Please press on in humility when differences arise, and always maintain a Christ-like love for your teammates as you serve them and with them. Please press on with the understanding that, although all co-laboring relationships are not permanent, the pattern is Biblically based and God-blessed.

Increase Your Faith

Ecclesiastes 4:9-12
9 Two are better than one;
because they have a good reward for their labour.
10 For if they fall, the one will lift up his fellow:
but woe to him that is alone when he falleth;
for he hath not another to help him up.
11 Again, if two lie together, then they have heat:
but how can one be warm alone?
12 And if one prevail against him, two shall withstand him;
and a threefold cord is not quickly broken.

Proverbs 11:14
14 Where no counsel is, the people fall:
but in the multitude of counsellors there is safety.

Proverbs 27:9, 17
9 Ointment and perfume rejoice the heart:
so doth the sweetness of a man's friend by hearty counsel.
17 Iron sharpeneth iron;
so a man sharpeneth the countenance of his friend.

Romans 12:3
3 For I say, through the grace given unto me,
to every man that is among you,
not to think of himself more highly than he ought to think;
but to think soberly,
according as God hath dealt to every man
the measure of faith.

Romans 12:18
18 If it be possible, as much as lieth in you,
live peaceably with all men.

Philippians 2:2-4

2 Fulfil ye my joy, that ye be likeminded,
having the same love, being of one accord, of one mind.
3 Let nothing be done through strife or vainglory;
but in lowliness of mind
let each esteem other better than themselves.
4 Look not every man on his own things,
but every man also on the things of others.

Galatians 6:3-5

3 For if a man think himself to be something,
when he is nothing,
he deceiveth himself.
4 But let every man prove his own work,
and then shall he have rejoicing in himself alone,
and not in another.
5 For every man shall bear his own burden.

I Peter 5:5-6

5 Likewise, ye younger, submit yourselves unto the elder.
Yea, all of you be subject one to another,
and be clothed with humility:
for God resisteth the proud, and giveth grace to the humble.
6 Humble yourselves therefore under the mighty hand of God,
that he may exalt you in due time:

Romans 10:17

So then faith cometh by hearing,
and hearing by the word of God.

Examples of Like Faith

Adam & Eve
Genesis 2:18

Moses
Exodus 18:14-26

Twelve Spies
Joshua & Caleb
Numbers 13:1-14:38

Mary and Martha
Luke 10:38-42

Romans 15:4
For whatsoever things were written aforetime
were written for our learning,
that we through patience and comfort of the scriptures
might have hope.

Chapter 13

FAMILY: YOUR MOST PRECIOUS POSSESSION

Joshua 24:15
And if it seem evil unto you to serve the LORD,
choose you this day whom ye will serve;
whether the gods which your fathers served
that were on the other side of the flood,
or the gods of the Amorites, in whose land ye dwell:
but as for me and my house, we will serve the LORD.

The Missionary's Experience

The missionary who has the extreme privilege of serving his Lord with his wife and children, often finds himself refreshed by sharing his joys and sorrows with those he loves and who love him. He also finds that due to the communication limitations and cultural differences with those around him, his family members are the only individuals with whom he can clearly share his heart and similar memories and traditions; therefore, they have become of the greatest value. However, he also recognizes that those most precious to him and who he would give his life to protect have been placed under extreme pressure and even danger because of their willingness to serve alongside him. They are called upon by God to bear the same physical and spiritual burdens he has surrendered himself to face. His wife carries the burdens of language, culture, climate, economics, health, discouragement, and attacks from others, all the while being far away from her family and friends, who would normally provide comfort and support. She is burdened with the great responsibility of helping her husband raise their children in a wicked and even dangerous environment. His precious children must face the difficulty of confusion and discouragement brought about by travel and of never really fitting in, of not having friends, and even being ridiculed simply because they are foreigners. He will need to teach and require of his children a level of maturity not expected of children years older, due to expectations of others and the sinful and dangerous situations they encounter on a daily basis. Added to these daily spiritual and physical burdens, he may be required to helplessly watch while one of these most precious to him face serious and long-term health concerns, which could be easily cared for at "home," but for which there is no treatment in his country of service.

Biblical Examples

Dear servant of God, Job's family suffered greatly because Job was a "righteous man," and God permitted his righteousness to be tested by Satan (Job 1). It was perhaps those very pressures that caused Job's wife to say to him, "*Dost thou still retain thine integrity? curse God, and die*" (Job 2:9). Job's wife was required to face the sorrow of the loss of their children and their financial security as well as helplessly watch as her husband was smitten "*with sore boils from the sole of his foot unto his crown. And he took him a potsherd to scrape himself withal; and he sat down among the ashes*" (Job 2:7-8). These pressures were overwhelming for Mrs. Job, just as they are many times for the family members of those Satan is trying to destroy. Although it is not often mentioned, Job's children also suffered because of Job's righteousness, as their lives were cut short by being crushed under the rubble of the oldest son's home (Job 1:18-19). Because of their father's commitment to the God of heaven, they were taken to Heaven early. However, after Job received the reports about his property and children, he "*arose, and rent his mantle, and shaved his head, and fell down upon the ground, and worshipped, And said,*

Naked came I out of my mother's womb, and naked shall I return thither: the LORD gave, and the LORD hath taken away; blessed be the name of the LORD. In all this Job sinned not, nor charged God foolishly" (Job 1:20-22). After listening to his wife's brokenness, he maintained his integrity before God as he replied to her, *"Thou speakest as one of the foolish women speaketh. What? shall we receive good at the hand of God, and shall we not receive evil? In all this did not Job sin with his lips"* (Job 2:10). Job was dedicated to serve God no matter what the personal cost or the cost to his family, and when his family began to doubt God's goodness, he quickly and clearly directed them to trust in God's sovereignty. As a servant of God, you must trust Him with your family. You must not allow Satan to win the victory over your faith because of the purposeful attacks he has made against your loved ones. Rather, you must remember that *"there hath no temptation taken you but such as is common to man: but God is faithful, who will not suffer you to be tempted above that ye are able; but will with the temptation also make a way to escape, that ye may be able to bear it"* (I Corinthians 10:13). In the future, there will be reason for you to *"greatly rejoice, though now for a season, if need be, ye are in heaviness through manifold temptations: that the trial of your faith, being much more precious than of gold that perisheth, though it be tried with fire, might be found unto praise and honour and glory at the appearing of Jesus Christ"* (I Peter 1:6-7).

Another example of the family being affected by the father's obedience to God is found in the life of Abraham. In Genesis 22:2, God commanded Abraham, saying, *"Take now thy son, thine only son Isaac, whom thou lovest, and get thee into the land of Moriah; and offer him there for a burnt offering upon one of the mountains which I will tell thee of."* Early the very next morning, Abraham began his journey of obedience with his son Isaac by his side (Genesis 22:3-5). After leaving the servants behind, Isaac helped his father by carrying the needed wood as they continued up the mountain (Genesis 22:6). As the father and son climbed together, Isaac asked questions. He said, *"My father: and he said, Here am I, my son. And he said, Behold the fire and the wood: but where is the lamb for a burnt offering?"* (Genesis 22:7). Abraham directed his son to have faith in God by saying, *"My son, God will provide himself a lamb for a burnt offering: so they went both of them together*" (Genesis 22:8). When they came to the place to which God had directed Abraham, he built an altar and prepared it for a blood sacrifice. Instead of finding a lamb, he followed God's will and "*bound Isaac his son, and laid him on the altar upon the wood*" (Genesis 22:9). Isaac, being a strong enough boy to carry the wood, was also obedient enough to permit his father to prepare him as the sacrifice. "*And Abraham stretched forth his hand, and took the knife to slay his son*" (Genesis 22:10). At every step of obedience Abraham took, his son Isaac was by his side and drawing closer to an early death, yet Abraham obeyed and Isaac with him. So, "*the angel of the LORD called unto him out of heaven, and said, Abraham, Abraham: and he said, Here am I. And he said, Lay not thine hand upon the lad, neither do thou any thing unto him: for now I know that thou fearest God, seeing thou hast not withheld thy son, thine only son from me*" (Genesis 22:11-12). Isaac had asked the question as to where the sacrificial animal would be found, and Abraham had told him that God would provide; and so He did, for "*Abraham lifted up his eyes, and looked, and behold behind him a ram caught in a thicket by his horns: and Abraham went and took the ram, and offered him up for a burnt offering in the stead of his son*" (Genesis 22:13). On this day, a father and son both enjoyed the awesome provision of God, because they were both willing to follow God's call upon the father's life. This event never damaged Isaac, but rather, Isaac went on to serve his father's God and was greatly blessed for doing so. As a servant of God, you must never seek to "protect" your children from God's will. You should enjoy the opportunity to accomplish God's will with your children by your side, so that they can learn by your example of serving the Only True God of heaven. You must say **publicly** and privately, "*As for me and my house, we will serve the LORD*" (Joshua 24:15).

Actual Events

I am very thankful to God that I have not yet been called upon to sacrifice the life of one of my children because of my call as a missionary. Although my wife and I have sorrowed over a miscarriage while in route to our first meeting on furlough, I realize that that loss cannot compare to standing over the grave of a precious son or daughter you have held and cared for. And although I have rushed my son of nine years to the hospital with serious and even life-threatening symptoms, I praise God that a few hours later I was able to drive him home again, and after weeks of doctor and specialist visits, he was given a clean bill of health. Through those hours and days, the possibility of losing my firstborn son became imminently real. Yet, through the remembrance of God's Word and the examples of those who have lost their spouse or child, I was drawn to pray earnestly for both my son's healing as well as God's strength to stay faithful no matter what the outcome (Hebrews 11:35-38). I also recognize that my family has been called upon to sacrifice in many other ways. I have watched my wife bear up under the extreme burden of loneliness, exhaustion, and untreated health needs. We, as a family, have shed tears together over the loss of our security and unfulfilled dreams, all of which have been sacrificed on the altar of God's will. And yet I know that the sacrifices of others have far exceeded ours. And there are those who will continue to face immeasurable losses in this life, all because of their obedience to their Lord and Savior, while maintaining their faith that *"the sufferings of this present time are not worthy to be compared with the glory which shall be revealed in us"* (Romans 8:18).

Biblical Exhortation

Dear servant of God, do not under-estimate the sacrifices you and your family may be called upon to make in order to serve your Savior. Your sacrifices and those of your family are great, and you must maintain a realistic view of them. Just as Abraham held a real knife in his hand, so the dangers you and your family face are real. You must allow those dangers to drive you to trust God more. You must remember Jesus Christ's words, as He said, *"He that loveth father or mother more than me is not worthy of me: and he that loveth son or daughter more than me is not worthy of me. And he that taketh not his cross, and followeth after me, is not worthy of me. He that findeth his life shall lose it: and he that loseth his life for my sake shall find it"* (Matthew 10:37-39).

Practical Participation

✎ **Missionary Candidate - Please prepare** yourself and your family for the reality of living in your new country by being informed about the difference you will face. Prepare yourself and each family member by learning Bible stories and passages to which you can easily retire when the burden of your new life and ministry become overwhelming. Please spend much time in prayer about the changes you will face, and ask God to prepare a clear path of protection and provision as you seek to obey His will for your life.

✎ **Missionary's Supporter - Please pray** diligently for each family member's spiritual, emotional, and physical well-being as they face many adjustments. Please pray that each family member will remember the greatness of their privilege to serve as their Savior's ambassadors. **Please provide** words and gifts of encouragement for each family member as they each sacrifice the "normal" life for the cause of Christ.

✎ **Missionary in Service - Please press on** as a family unit, unified by Christ, for Christ, and in order to share Christ with those you have been called to serve together. Please press on knowing that God cares for each family member equally and will not neglect to care for them personally. Please press on, trusting God's protection from both physical and spiritual dangers, as you serve Him as his ambassador away from the protection of "home."

Increase Your Faith

Genesis 18:19
19 For I know him,
that he will command his children
and his household after him,
and they shall keep the way of the LORD,
to do justice and judgment;
that the LORD may bring upon Abraham
that which he hath spoken of him.

Deuteronomy 6:2, 5-9
2 That thou mightest fear the LORD thy God,
to keep all his statutes and his commandments,
which I command thee, thou, and thy son, and thy son's son,
all the days of thy life;
and that thy days may be prolonged.
5 And thou shalt love the LORD thy God with all thine heart,
and with all thy soul, and with all thy might.
6 And these words, which I command thee this day,
shall be in thine heart:
7 And thou shalt teach them diligently unto thy children,
and shalt talk of them when thou sittest in thine house,
and when thou walkest by the way,
and when thou liest down, and when thou risest up.
8 And thou shalt bind them for a sign upon thine hand,
and they shall be as frontlets between thine eyes.
9 And thou shalt write them upon the posts of thy house,
and on thy gates.

Psalm 101:2
2 I will behave myself wisely in a perfect way.
O when wilt thou come unto me?
I will walk within my house with a perfect heart.

Psalm 127:1-5

1 Except the LORD build the house,
they labour in vain that build it:
except the LORD keep the city,
the watchman waketh but in vain.
2 It is vain for you to rise up early, to sit up late,
to eat the bread of sorrows:
for so he giveth his beloved sleep.
3 Lo, children are an heritage of the LORD:
and the fruit of the womb is his reward.
4 As arrows are in the hand of a mighty man;
so are children of the youth.
5 Happy is the man that hath his quiver full of them:
they shall not be ashamed,
but they shall speak with the enemies in the gate.

Joshua 24:14-15

14 Now therefore fear the LORD,
and serve him in sincerity and in truth:
and put away the gods
which your fathers served
on the other side of the flood, and in Egypt;
and serve ye the LORD.
15 And if it seem evil unto you to serve the LORD,
choose you this day whom ye will serve;
whether the gods which your fathers served
that were on the other side of the flood,
or the gods of the Amorites, in whose land ye dwell:
but as for me and my house, we will serve the LORD.

Matthew 10:37-39

*37 He that loveth father or mother more than me
is not worthy of me:
and he that loveth son or daughter more than me
is not worthy of me.
38 And he that taketh not his cross, and followeth after me,
is not worthy of me.
39 He that findeth his life shall lose it:
and he that loseth his life for my sake shall find it.*

Romans 10:17
So then faith cometh by hearing,
and hearing by the word of God.

Examples of Like Faith

Noah & His Sons
Genesis 6:1-9:19

Aquila & Priscilla
Acts 18:1-2, 18-19, 26
I Corinthians 16:19
II Timothy 4:19

Philip & His Daughters
Acts 21:8-9

Romans 15:4
For whatsoever things were written aforetime
were written for our learning,
that we through patience and comfort of the scriptures
might have hope.

Chapter 14

MISSIONARY OR MOOCHINARY?

Proverbs 30:8-9
Remove far from me vanity and lies:
give me neither poverty nor riches;
feed me with food convenient for me:
Lest I be full, and deny thee, and say,
Who is the LORD?
or lest I be poor, and steal,
and take the name of my God in vain.

The Missionary's Experience

The missionary's financial situation can be one of the greatest distractions and discouragements to his ministry. As he arrives in his new country, begins to establish his home, and start his ministry, it is very probable that he will spend in just a few weeks the thousands of dollars he had taken years to raise and save. Most likely, he will also find that the economic situation of his new country has changed since making his budget and that, although he left his homeland supported 100 percent, he now does not have an adequate amount to live and minister with because he now has only 85-95 percent of what his budget should have been. Then, as he more thoroughly investigates the best location for a building to house his ministry, he finds that the cost of property and utilities far exceeds what he had anticipated. Although he has seen God clearly work to supply his needs through his ministry training, deputation process, and in reaching his goal of living and ministering on the foreign field, he may begin to doubt how he can adequately minister without the funds needed to purchase simple ministry supplies such as tracts, Bibles, hymnals, children's materials, etc. Although he may be able to locate these materials (which, can be a task in and of itself) and pay for the purchase price, he cannot afford the ever increasing expense of shipping and handling. With no other option before him, and after reluctantly receiving admonition from others, he humbly begins to share his needs with fellow believers while battling the unrealistic expectations placed upon him to live by "faith" and therefore live and minister in poverty and debt. For this reason, the missionary will regularly seek for ways to eliminate personal comforts and needs so as to adequately minister to the nationals while protecting himself from being considered a "moochinary" (moocher + missionary). The missionary who sets his heart upon being a good steward of God's unsearchable riches in heaven will often find himself as a steward of pennies in this world. This pressure will most definitely have great effects upon the man, his family, and his ministry-effectiveness over the years and could become the final blow to his longevity in ministry.

Biblical Examples

Dear servant of God, remember the words of our Lord Jesus Christ when He said, *"Foxes have holes, and birds of the air have nests; but the Son of man hath not where to lay his head"* (Luke 9:58). Jesus lived a life of great need and poverty even though He was the Son of God and the Creator of all things (Colossians 1:15-16). While living on this earth, He depended on His heavenly Father and the generosity of others, and He often made His resting place and residence in the homes of His friends (Luke 10:38, John 11:1-12:8). When there was need for food to feed the five-thousand he asked a small boy to sacrifice his lunch (John 6:5-13). And when He was required to pay His taxes, He said to Peter, *"Go thou to the sea, and cast an hook, and take up the fish that first cometh up; and when thou hast opened his mouth, thou shalt find a piece of money: that take, and give unto them for me and thee"* (Matthew 17:27). Jesus Christ was a man of no known wealth or belongings. Even at the end of His life, the solders did not gamble over his land or gold; they "*took his garments, and made four parts, to every soldier a part; and also his coat: now the coat was without seam, woven from the top throughout. They said therefore among themselves, Let us not rend it, but cast lots for it, whose it shall be*" (John 19:23-24). And yet it was Jesus Christ who taught His followers to "*take no thought for your life, what ye shall eat, or what ye shall drink; nor yet for your body, what ye shall put on. Is not the life more than meat, and the body than raiment? . . . Therefore take no thought, saying, What shall we eat? or, What shall we drink? or, Wherewithal shall we be clothed? (For after all these things do the Gentiles seek:) for your heavenly Father knoweth that ye have need of all these things. But seek ye first the kingdom of God, and his righteousness; and all these things shall be added unto you*" (Matthew 6:25-33).

This same principle was taught by Paul as he said, "*Perverse disputings of men of corrupt minds, and destitute of the truth, supposing that gain is godliness: from such withdraw thyself. But godliness with contentment is great gain. For we brought nothing into this world, and it is certain we can carry nothing out. And having food and raiment let us be therewith content*" (I Timothy 6:5-8). Paul understood poverty. He understood the lack of the "necessities of life" as he told the church at Corinth, "*Even unto this present hour we both hunger, and thirst, and are naked, and are buffeted, and have no certain dwelling place; and labour, working with our own hands: being reviled, we bless; being persecuted, we suffer it*" (I Corinthians 4:11-12). Paul also understood the humility necessary to depend upon other believers as the church at Philippi "*sent once and again unto my [his] necessity*" (Philippians 4:16). He gratefully said to those believers, "*But I have all, and abound: I am full, having received of Epaphroditus the things which were sent from you, an odour of a sweet smell, a sacrifice acceptable, wellpleasing to God*" (Philippians 4:18). Paul was able to live and minister while in great need because he had "*learned, in whatsoever state I am, therewith to be content. I know both how to be abased, and I know how to abound: every where and in all things I am instructed both to be full and to be hungry, both to abound and to suffer need. I can do all things through Christ which strengtheneth*" (Philippians 4:11-13).

Actual Events

As I made preparation to depart for my field of service, I took seriously the need to count the financial costs of accomplishing God's ministry (Luke 14:28-32). And so I prayed earnestly and worked diligently to establish an adequate yet reasonable budget based upon the best information I could gather. I then prayed and waited for God's provision of that budget before setting off to start my new life and ministry. Yet, within the first year on the field, the water bill doubled, the electric bill doubled to tripled, and the government implemented for the first time a 7 percent sales tax. With these expenses increasing, as well as the constant increase to the cost of living, I discovered very quickly that our budget was not even close to accurate. There was only one option; we needed to trust God to make up the shortfall. He began to do so through individual periodic gifts and finally more regular promised support. I will admit that I have never again reached 100 percent of my needed budget since that first year (even after a furlough), but I have always had God's supply at the exact time of my need. And so I pray that God will *"remove far from me vanity and lies: give me neither poverty nor riches; feed me with food convenient for me: lest I be full, and deny thee, and say, Who is the LORD? or lest I be poor, and steal, and take the name of my God in vain"* (Proverbs 30:8-9).

Biblical Exhortation

Dear servant of God, the reality of financial burdens have been experienced by God's people throughout all time and in every part of the world (Acts 11:27-30). Yet He has never let them down. He has always provided for them in accordance to His great love for them and wisdom of knowing what is best for them. As you seek to proclaim God's Word, you will have financial and physical needs. But be assured that *"your heavenly Father knoweth that ye have need of all these things"* (Matthew 6:30). And always remember that your heavenly father is much better than any earthly father. And Jesus said, *"For every one that asketh receiveth; and he that seeketh findeth; and to him that knocketh it shall be opened. If a son shall ask bread of any of you that is a father, will he give him a stone? or if he ask a fish, will he for a fish give him a serpent? Or if he shall ask an egg, will he offer him a scorpion? If ye then, being evil, know how to give good gifts unto your children: how much more shall your heavenly Father give the Holy Spirit to them that ask him?"* (Luke 11:10-12).

Practical Participation

✎ **Missionary Candidate - Please prepare** yourself well for the known budgeting and supply needs you will have in order to accomplish your ministry. And do not take for granted that you will always have enough if you have not investigated correctly and diligently asked God to supply. Prepare yourself by beginning now to live within what is necessary, instead of enjoying the riches you may have available now but won't have later. Humbly prepare yourself to be a recipient of God's and other's generosity later by displaying that same generosity to those in need around you right now.

✎ **Missionary's Supporter - Please pray** for wisdom and protection for your missionary in using the provision he currently has. Please pray that God will also provide for those shortfalls that may come unexpectedly or outside of the missionary's control. **Please provide** for your missionary to live a life as you would desire to live and do not expect him to have any less of a standard of living than you would expect for yourself. Provide for ministry needs and opportunities so that he can continue to expand the Gospel ministry to new people and places.

✎ **Missionary in Service - Please press on** in faith, knowing that God knows your every personal and ministry need. Please press on by not trusting in your supporters but in the God who provides for them to provide for you. Please press on in looking for new ministry opportunities no matter what the cost, and then turn to God and ask Him to show His will by providing for every detail of your new ministry adventure.

Increase Your Faith

Psalm 20:7
7 Some trust in chariots, and some in horses:
but we will remember the name of the LORD our God.

Proverbs 3:9-10
9 Honour the LORD with thy substance,
and with the firstfruits of all thine increase:
10 So shall thy barns be filled with plenty,
and thy presses shall burst out with new wine.

Matthew 6:24-34
24 No man can serve two masters:
for either he will hate the one, and love the other;
or else he will hold to the one, and despise the other.
Ye cannot serve God and mammon.
25 Therefore I say unto you,
Take no thought for your life, what ye shall eat,
or what ye shall drink;
nor yet for your body, what ye shall put on.
Is not the life more than meat, and the body than raiment?
26 Behold the fowls of the air:
for they sow not, neither do they reap,
nor gather into barns;
yet your heavenly Father feedeth them.
Are ye not much better than they?
27 Which of you by taking thought
can add one cubit unto his stature?
28 And why take ye thought for raiment?
Consider the lilies of the field, how they grow;
they toil not, neither do they spin:
29 And yet I say unto you,
That even Solomon in all his glory
was not arrayed like one of these.

*30 Wherefore, if God so clothe the grass of the field,
which to day is, and to morrow is cast into the oven,
shall he not much more clothe you, O ye of little faith?
31 Therefore take no thought, saying, What shall we eat?
or, What shall we drink?
or, Wherewithal shall we be clothed?
32 (For after all these things do the Gentiles seek:)
for your heavenly Father knoweth that ye have need
of all these things.
33 But seek ye first the kingdom of God,
and his righteousness;
and all these things shall be added unto you.
34 Take therefore no thought for the morrow:
for the morrow shall take thought for the things of itself.
Sufficient unto the day is the evil thereof.*

Luke 6:38

*38 Give, and it shall be given unto you;
good measure, pressed down,
and shaken together, and running over,
shall men give into your bosom.
For with the same measure that ye mete
withal it shall be measured to you again.*

I Timothy 6:3-9

*6 But godliness with contentment is great gain.
7 For we brought nothing into this world,
and it is certain we can carry nothing out.
8 And having food and raiment
let us be therewith content.
9 But they that will be rich fall into temptation and a snare,
and into many foolish and hurtful lusts,
which drown men in destruction and perdition.*

James 4:1-3

1 From whence come wars and fightings among you?
come they not hence,
even of your lusts that war in your members?
2 Ye lust, and have not:
ye kill, and desire to have, and cannot obtain:
ye fight and war, yet ye have not, because ye ask not.
3 Ye ask, and receive not, because ye ask amiss,
that ye may consume it upon your lusts.

Romans 10:17
So then faith cometh by hearing,
and hearing by the word of God.

Examples of Like Faith

Widow Women and Elijah
I Kings 17:9-27

Israel
Nehemiah 9:19-22

Romans 15:4
For whatsoever things were written aforetime
were written for our learning,
that we through patience and comfort of the scriptures
might have hope.

Chapter 15

NO REST FOR THE WEARY

Isaiah 40:29-31
He giveth power to the faint;
and to them that have no might he increaseth strength.
Even the youths shall faint and be weary,
and the young men shall utterly fall:
But they that wait upon the LORD shall renew their strength;
they shall mount up with wings as eagles;
they shall run, and not be weary;
and they shall walk, and not faint.

The Missionary's Experience

As the missionary completes each task required to get him to his field of service, establish his new home, find a location for and start his new ministry, all within a relatively short period of time, he will find that his energy level produced from the adrenaline of the excitement of finally being able to do what he had dreamed about, will come up short. He quickly recognizes that the tasks before him require that he not sprint to the finish but rather that he take each day and each task as if he were running a spiritual cross-country race in which he is to "**run with patience the race that is set before us [him]**" while "*looking unto Jesus the author and finisher of our faith*" (Hebrews 12:1-2). Throughout his ministry journey, he finds many exhausting mountains to climb, but he will also find helpful times of rest as he coasts back down the other side. He enjoys the great mountaintop experience that comes with each spiritual victory while facing the discouraging effects of the valleys. With each of these experiences, he continually finds himself battling the frailty of his flesh as he becomes weary in the work, only to find that there is little or no rest for the weary. During this adjustment period on the field, he finds himself constantly tired, even after a "normal" night's rest, not realizing that he really is not resting comfortably due to his awkward surroundings. He finds that simple tasks that he accomplished without thought in the past, such as running to the store or cutting the grass, now drain him of an entire day's worth of energy. What he does not realize is that his body and mind and soul are working overtime all the time. They are attempting to adjust to the newness of the climate, culture, language, surroundings, etc. Added to all of these physical changes are the spiritual battles that he had never encountered before but that Satan will use to try to eliminate his effectiveness in spreading the Gospel. While these spiritual battles may be unseen, the Scripture is clear that the missionary must *"be strong in the Lord, and in the power of his might"* because human strength is not adequate, as he *"wrestles not against flesh and blood, but against principalities, against powers, against the rulers of the darkness of this world, against spiritual wickedness in high places"* (Ephesians 6:10, 12).

Biblical Examples

Dear servant of God, human weakness and frailty is normal, *"for he knoweth our frame; he remembereth that we are dust"* (Psalm 101:14). King David was so exhausted after fighting the Philistines that *"his hand was weary, and his hand clave unto the sword"* (II Samuel 23:10). Jesus and his disciples were so busy in the ministry that *"there were many coming and going, and they had no leisure so much as to eat"* (Mark 6:31). And when Jesus said, *"Come ye yourselves apart into a desert place, and rest a while . . . the people saw them departing, and many knew him, and ran afoot thither out of all cities, and outwent them, and came together unto him. And Jesus, when he came out, saw much people, and was moved with compassion toward them, because they were as sheep not having a shepherd: and he began to teach them many things"* (Mark 6:31-34).

The amount of work needed for God's ministry cannot be underestimated. It is a responsibility that consumes much time and energy from those who are committed to accomplish it correctly (II Corinthians 11:28). The Apostle Paul knew firsthand of this weariness in ministry as he experienced *"labours more abundant, in stripes above measure, in prisons more frequent, in deaths oft. Of the Jews five times received I forty stripes save one. Thrice was I beaten with rods, once was I stoned, thrice I suffered shipwreck, a night and a day I have been in the deep; in journeyings often, in perils of waters, in perils of robbers, in perils by mine own countrymen, in perils by the heathen, in perils in the city, in perils in the wilderness, in perils in the sea, in perils among false brethren; in weariness and painfulness, in watchings often, in hunger and thirst, in fastings often, in cold and nakedness. Beside those things that are without, that which cometh upon me daily, the care of all the churches"* (II Corinthians 11:23-28). Yet he wrote, *"Therefore seeing we have this ministry, as we have received mercy, we faint not. . . . But if our gospel be hid, it is hid to them that are lost"* (II Corinthians 4:1-3).

Paul's commitment to ministry was based on the mercy he received from God. And that mercy helped Him recognize that *"God, who commanded the light to shine out of darkness, hath shined in our hearts, to give the light of the knowledge of the glory of God in the face of Jesus Christ. But we have this treasure in earthen vessels, that the excellency of the power may be of God, and not of us. We are troubled on every side, yet not distressed; we are perplexed, but not in despair; persecuted, but not forsaken; cast down, but not destroyed; always bearing about in the body the dying of the Lord Jesus, that the life also of Jesus might be made manifest in our body. For we which live are alway delivered unto death for Jesus' sake, that the life also of Jesus might be made manifest in our mortal flesh"* (II Corinthians 4:6-11).

Paul lovingly continues to share with the Corinthian believers that all of his suffering and weariness in ministry was for their *"sakes, that the abundant grace might through the thanksgiving of many redound to the glory of God. For which cause we faint not; but though our outward man perish, yet the inward man is renewed day by day"* (II Corinthians 4:15-16). Paul realized that his ministry was taking a toll physically on his body, but he was willing to sacrifice physically so that other believers could benefit spiritually. He did not make this sacrifice in his own strength but by allowing God to empower his inner man daily so that his outward man could continue his ministry to others. This level of dedication is needed of each minister of God no matter his age or experience. No minister of God should succumb to the "Elijah syndrome" in which, after great energy is spent and even greater spiritual victories have been won, the spiritual leader finds himself overcome with weariness and discouragement (I Kings 18:7-19:4). But rather, as the *"outward man"* begins to perish, he must rely on God for rest and sustenance and then look to God for a renewed purpose and power to accomplish God's future plans for ministry (I Kings 19:5-18).

Actual Events

The level of stamina and health are particular to each missionary. As I grew up, I was always known as a "go-getter." I was even given the nickname, "Spark Plug," in sports. However, that level of energy changed after a few health concerns appeared years before I left for my mission field. But, although I didn't have all the pep of a teenager, I still rarely slowed down. It was not uncommon for me to work twelve- to fourteen-hour days in construction projects and yet still stay up late to study at home. But almost immediately after arriving on my field of service, my energy level was cut in half. I became concerned that I had been sick and even tried a few multi-vitamins and health shakes to recoup the energy I was lacking, but nothing seemed to help. As no other real symptoms appeared, I realized that my weariness was the direct result of the new climate, culture, language, and spiritual pressures within. With time I began to see my energy level reappear. However, a few years later I began to face other health concerns, which once again had taken the pep out of my step, and yet there was no time for relaxation or rest. The ministry demands required flexibility and focus both in hard physical labor as well as in deep, concentrated study. During these years of ministry, I felt the physical drain of being available to minister to God's people with *"humility of mind, and with many tears, and temptations*" both "*publickly, and from house to house*" as I attempted "*to declare unto you [them] all the counsel of God*" by being faithful "*to warn every one night and day with tears*" (Acts 20:19-27). The longer I participate in this style of ministry, the more I recognize that it cannot be accomplished with man's might but that I must depend on the mercy that I have received so that I "*faint not*" (II Corinthians 4:15).

Biblical Exhortation

Dear servant of God, do not be surprised by the weariness you feel. Rather, commit yourself in your weariness to look to God for His strength to carry on faithfully. Remember that your "*God is not unrighteous to forget your work and labour of love, which ye have shewed toward his name, in that ye have ministered to the saints, and do minister*" (Hebrews 6:10). Continue to fight the spiritual battles by being "*strong in the Lord, and in the power of his might*" (Ephesians 6:10). And "*be not weary in well doing*" (Galatians 6:9, II Thessalonians 3:13). "*Hast thou not known? hast thou not heard, that the everlasting God, the LORD, the Creator of the ends of the earth, fainteth not, neither is weary? there is no searching of his understanding. He giveth power to the faint; and to them that have no might he increaseth strength. Even the youths shall faint and be weary, and the young men shall utterly fall: But they that wait upon the LORD shall renew their strength; they shall mount up with wings as eagles; they shall run, and not be weary; and they shall walk, and not faint*" (Isaiah 40:28-31).

Practical Participation

✎ Missionary Candidate - Please prepare yourself by making sure you are both physically and spiritually ready to serve God wherever He might send you. Prepare by planning well for your initial adjustments to your new environment so that weariness does not lead to discouragement.

✎ Missionary's Supporter - Please pray for energy for your missionary as he struggles to fulfill his ministry responsibilities and cope with his medical conditions. Please pray that, though weary, your missionary will never fail to fulfill God's perfect will in His plentiful strength. **Please provide** the opportunity and provision for your missionary to take the time he needs to rest and recoup both while he is on his field of service as well as when he is visiting his supporters at home. Provide encouraging and wise counsel about his health concerns and his level of responsibilities, always remembering that his options may be very different from what you are accustomed to.

✎ Missionary in Service - Please press on with a realistic understanding of your physical limitation. Press on with a humble dependence on God's strength for each task you seek to accomplish. Please press on by wise participation in only those activities and ministries that are really God's will for your life and ministry.

Increase Your Faith

Psalm 27:13-14
13 I had fainted,
unless I had believed to see the goodness of the LORD
in the land of the living.
14 Wait on the LORD: be of good courage,
and he shall strengthen thine heart:
wait, I say, on the LORD.

II Corinthians 1:8-10
8 For we would not, brethren,
have you ignorant of our trouble which came to us in Asia,
that we were pressed out of measure, above strength,
insomuch that we despaired even of life:
9 But we had the sentence of death in ourselves,
that we should not trust in ourselves,
but in God which raiseth the dead:
10 Who delivered us from so great a death, and doth deliver:
in whom we trust that he will yet deliver us;

II Corinthians 4:1, 16
1 Therefore seeing we have this ministry,
as we have received mercy,
we faint not;
16 For which cause we faint not;
but though our outward man perish,
yet the inward man is renewed day by day.

II Corinthians 12:10
10 Therefore I take pleasure in infirmities,
in reproaches, in necessities, in persecutions,
in distresses for Christ's sake:
for when I am weak, then am I strong.

Galatians 6:9-10

9 And let us not be weary in well doing:
for in due season we shall reap, if we faint not.
10 As we have therefore opportunity,
let us do good unto all men,
especially unto them who are of the household of faith.

Philippians 4:11-13

11 Not that I speak in respect of want:
for I have learned, in whatsoever state I am,
therewith to be content.
12 I know both how to be abased,
and I know how to abound:
every where and in all things I am instructed
both to be full and to be hungry,
both to abound and to suffer need.
13 I can do all things through Christ
which strengtheneth me.

Romans 10:17
So then faith cometh by hearing,
and hearing by the word of God.

Examples of Like Faith

Moses
Genesis 17:11-12

David
II Samuel 23:10

The Church of Ephesus
Revelation 2:1-7

Romans 15:4
For whatsoever things were written aforetime
were written for our learning,
that we through patience and comfort of the scriptures
might have hope.

Chapter 16

WHO? WHAT? WHEN? WHERE? HOW?

Proverbs 3:5-6
Trust in the LORD with all thine heart;
and lean not unto thine own understanding.
In all thy ways acknowledge him,
and he shall direct thy paths.

The Missionary's Experience

The missionary's decision to surrender all in order to proclaim the Word of God around the world does not end the missionary's decision-making process. But rather it has just begun. This single choice has thrust the missionary into a life-long process of searching for God's will by asking: Who should I minister to? What should I do to minister? When should I start to minister? Where should I focus my ministry? And how should I go about accomplishing my ministry? Even the simplest of responsibilities, such as evangelism, will involve much time, research, and prayer so that he can find the correct materials (the correct message clearly presented in the correct language), the correct acceptable method, the correct timing, the correct area specifically prepared by God to receive him, etc. Along with the major decision to minister, he will need to wisely decide in which specific ministry opportunities he will spend his time, energy, and resources, as there will be many, and each one will beg for his full attention. He will also need to wisely decide how to implement or reject his personal ideas and desires along with the suggestions of others who may or may not understand his ministry's circumstances nor the culture of his people. As his ministry continues through the years, he will most likely need to make major decisions about the expansion or even movement of his ministry. Correct timing of his furloughs or even permanent departure from the ministry, needs to be based upon the true spiritual maturity of the believers who will carry on the work in his absence.

Biblical Examples

Dear minister of God, your search for God's will in ministry has only begun. You need to be dependent upon Him not only to know the task you are to perform but also the manner in which you are to accomplish it. Gideon knew that God had called him to rescue Israel from the eminent danger of the Midianites (Judges 6:1-24). In that very call, God declared something about Gideon that would only be displayed through his obedience. He *"said unto him, The LORD is with thee, thou mighty man of valour"* (Judges 6:12). Gideon needed to take specific steps of faith in order to prepare himself for and accomplish each task along the way. First, Gideon was commanded by God to show his obedience by destroying his father's altars to false gods, and Gideon obeyed (Judges 6:25-32). Then Gideon requested that God would confirm His will through providing two miracles with a fleece. And God graciously performed his request, proving His power and presence (Judges 6:34-40). And in the final preparation for the attack, God commanded Gideon to change his plan of attack from using 32,000 men to attacking with only 300 by using a specific elimination process provided by God Himself (Judges 7:1-8). God then reassured Gideon of His personal protection and victory by providing an opportunity to hear the conversation of one of the enemy soldiers who was fearful (Judges 7:9-15). And then, against all odds, in an unconventional military move, Gideon attacked the Midianites at night with only a lantern, a pitcher, and a trumpet in the hand of each of his soldiers, and he won the victory (Judges 7:16-25). The decision-making process to take Gideon from being told he would win the victory over the Midianites to actually achieving the victory was lengthy, and it is very similar to a missionary's life and ministry. He is to set out knowing he has the victory, but he must take steps along the way to prove himself to be obedient to God and to grow in his faith in God so that God can one day provide the seemingly impossible.

The Apostle Paul also experienced the need to find and follow God's will throughout his life and ministry. He knew that his calling was to go to the gentiles, *"to open their eyes, and to turn them from darkness to light, and from the power of Satan unto God, that they may receive forgiveness of sins, and inheritance among them which are sanctified by faith that is in me"* (Acts 26:18). And he knew that he had been sent by the will of God, as *"the Holy Ghost said, Separate me Barnabas and Saul for the work whereunto I have called them. . . . So they, being sent forth by the Holy Ghost, departed"* (Acts 13:2-3). Yet on occasion, Paul's intended plans for ministry were not realized because the Holy Spirit redirected him so that he could minister to others. This is exactly what took place as he was *"forbidden of the Holy Ghost to preach the word in Asia"* (Acts 16:6). And then again as he attempted to go to Bithynia, *"the Spirit suffered them not"* (Acts 16:7). Little did he know that God was purposefully directing his ministry trips to place him in the correct location to make the most direct route to Macedonia after he received a vision of a man in Macedonia asking for his help (Acts 16:9-10). And so, knowing God's will, he *"immediately . . . endeavored to go into Macedonia, assuredly gathering that the Lord had called us [them] for to preach the gospel unto them"* (Acts 16:10).

On another occasion, however, Paul admitted that other spiritual powers were attempting to hinder his ministry in Thessalonica: *"Wherefore we would have come unto you, even I Paul, once and again; but Satan hindered us"* (I Thessalonians 2:18). On one occasion, Paul's plans were prevented and redirected by God. On another occasion, they were prevented by Satan. On still another occasion, they were simply delayed until God's perfect timing and other ministry opportunities were fulfilled. Such a delay is exactly what took place with Paul's plans to minister in Rome. He described his situation to the believers by saying, *"Now I would not have you ignorant, brethren, that oftentimes I purposed to come unto you, (but was let hitherto,) that I might have some fruit among you also, even as among other Gentiles*" (Romans 1:13). Later, he adds to his explanation by saying "*Yea, so have I strived to preach the gospel, not where Christ was named, lest I should build upon another man's foundation: . . . For which cause also I have been much hindered from coming to you*" (Romans 15:20-22). But Acts 19:21 reveals that he continued to make plans to go to Rome: "*After these things were ended, Paul purposed in the spirit, when he had passed through Macedonia and Achaia, to go to Jerusalem, saying, After I have been there, I must also see Rome.*" Finally, about 2-3 years after he wrote the book of Romans, Paul did arrive in Rome but very differently than he had originally intended. He arrived in Rome under arrest and chained to a Roman guard after experiencing a ship wreck on the isle of Melita (Acts 27:1-16). Paul was a man of constant focus on the ministry, while always depending upon the will of God for how and when He should fulfil that ministry. He was always willing to live by James' instruction: "*If the Lord will, we shall live, and do this, or that*" (James 4:15).

Actual Events

My personal ministry plans changed just months before I arrived on my field of service. It was during language school that I found out that my future, veteran co-workers would be changing their ministry location. They had been ministering in the area of the country where I had always had a burden and that we had been sharing with people for years that we were going to be serving. But through a chain of decisions made by others, I quickly found my ministry plans falling apart. Not only did this mean that we would be further away from other missionaries I already knew, I also learned very quickly that I would be ministering in an area that had a very unique culture, accent, and even resistance to outsiders. The first years of ministry were difficult and discouraging. I simply could not shake my desire to be in the other town, and as problems arose, it was easy to think that if we had been where I had originally planned, I would be so much better off. So I began to earnestly pray for God to open the door for a change of location or a change of my heart. I began to ask questions of other missionaries and make survey trips to the other areas of the country. I even had another veteran missionary ask me to co-labor with him. But God continually prevented the financial details to be worked out. At the same time, my co-workers took a furlough during which time I was privileged to care for the work of the ministry and the people by myself. It was during this time that God continued to close the door for me to move to another town and began to knit my heart to the small group of individuals right where I was already ministering. God had directed, redirected, and then provided His confirmation to accept the entire responsibility of the ministry just a short time later as my co-laborers chose to retire. These steps were not easy. The disappointments were real and at times nearly consumed me. But as I continued to give them back to God by delighting myself in Him, He changed my heart so that He could then in turn *"give thee [me] the desires of thine [my] heart"* (Psalm 37:4).

Biblical Exhortation

Dear servant of God, you must never take your ministry plans into your own hands. You must never move before God directs, nor can you hesitate when your time for departure is revealed. You must always be firm in your dedication to ministry and be flexible in God's hands as to where, how, and to whom to minister. The choices you make to go or stay, visit this street or go to the next, begin an outreach today or wait until next month must all be dependent upon the perfect will of God. You must dedicate yourself to be a good (godly) man, while trusting that *"the steps of a good man are ordered by the LORD: and he delighteth in his way"* (Psalm 37:23).

Practical Participation

✎ **Missionary Candidate - Please prepare** yourself for unexpected changes to your ministry. Prepare yourself by living one day at a time, constantly looking to your heavenly Father for His specific and perfect will for your large decisions as well as the seemingly insignificant ones.

✎ **Missionary's Supporter - Please pray** for your missionary as he is constantly being forced into decision-making situations. Please pray that he will be firm in his dedication to ministry and yet flexible in his plans for ministry. **Please provide** wise and prayerful counsel as your missionary shares his future ministry plans. Also, provide a kind and flexible spirit when your missionary's plans seem to change.

✎ **Missionary in Service - Please press on** with God's will no matter where it may take you. Do not allow a change in your plans to discourage you or distract you from consistent ministry wherever God leads you. Please press on knowing that the changes you encounter are part of God's kind directing hand to show you what is best for you and where you can serve Him best.

Increase Your Faith

Genesis 24:27
*27 And he said,
Blessed be the LORD God of my master Abraham,
who hath not left destitute my master
of his mercy and his truth:
I being in the way,
the LORD led me to the house of my master's brethren.*

Psalm 37:4-5
*4 Delight thyself also in the LORD;
and he shall give thee the desires of thine heart.
5 Commit thy way unto the LORD;
trust also in him; and he shall bring it to pass.*

Psalm 37:23-24
*23 The steps of a good man are ordered by the LORD:
and he delighteth in his way.
24 Though he fall, he shall not be utterly cast down:
for the LORD upholdeth him with his hand.*

Romans 15:32
*32 That I may come unto you with joy by the will of God,
and may with you be refreshed.*

I John 2:17
*17 And the world passeth away, and the lust thereof:
but he that doeth the will of God abideth for ever.*

James 4:13-15

13 Go to now, ye that say,
To day or to morrow we will go into such a city,
and continue there a year,
and buy and sell, and get gain:
14 Whereas ye know not what shall be on the morrow.
For what is your life?
It is even a vapour, that appeareth for a little time,
and then vanisheth away.
15 For that ye ought to say,
If the Lord will, we shall live, and do this, or that.

Romans 10:17
So then faith cometh by hearing,
and hearing by the word of God.

Examples of Like Faith

Abraham's Servant
Genesis 24:1-67

David
I Samuel 16:1-13, 23:1-16

Elijah & Naaman
II Kings 5:1-16

Peter
Acts 10:1-48

Romans 15:4
For whatsoever things were written aforetime
were written for our learning,
that we through patience and comfort of the scriptures
might have hope.

Chapter 17

THE BURDEN OF REJECTION

II Corinthians 12:15
And I will very gladly spend and be spent for you;
though the more abundantly I love you,
the less I be loved,

The Missionary's Experience

One of the greatest burdens a missionary faces is personal rejection. A missionary often finds himself under a huge burden as he attempts to establish his new life and ministry in a foreign country with people who consider him an "outsider." No matter how hard the missionary tries to change his appearance, implement native practices, eat native food, and speak the native language, he will always be "different" and therefore always subject to the rejection of those who do not like "different" things. For most missionaries, this would be bearable if this rejection were only expressed by the unbelieving. But when that same missionary has been rejected by those he has evangelized and taught for years by the sacrificial giving of himself, his time, and his resources, the rejection can become devastating. Throughout years of ministry, the missionary begins to make himself vulnerable by sharing his life, his belongings, his dreams, etc., with those to whom God sent him to serve. As he seeks to allow those in his ministry to become his new family, it is often those very same dear ones who will quickly take advantage of him and his sacrifices by rejecting both him and his teaching when a disagreement arises or sin is desired more than truth. This rejection is often unmatched by fellowship with other ministers or comforting words from extended family and friends because he has left them all thousands of miles away in sacrifice for the very ones who are now rejecting him. The missionary's feeling of total and complete devastation is best described by David in Psalm 55:1-7, 12-14, 20-21, where he said, *"Give ear to my prayer, O God; and hide not thyself from my supplication. Attend unto me, and hear me: I mourn in my complaint, and make a noise; because of the voice of the enemy, because of the oppression of the wicked: for they cast iniquity upon me, and in wrath they hate me. My heart is sore pained within me: and the terrors of death are fallen upon me. Fearfulness and trembling are come upon me, and horror hath overwhelmed me. And I said, Oh that I had wings like a dove! for then would I fly away, and be at rest. Lo, then would I wander far off, and remain in the wilderness. Selah. I would hasten my escape from the windy storm and tempest. For it was not an enemy that reproached me; then I could have borne it: neither was it he that hated me that did magnify himself against me; then I would have hid myself from him: but it was thou, a man mine equal, my guide, and mine acquaintance. We took sweet counsel together, and walked unto the house of God in company. He hath put forth his hands against such as be at peace with him: he hath broken his covenant. The words of his mouth were smoother than butter, but war was in his heart: his words were softer than oil, yet were they drawn swords."*

Biblical Examples

Dear servant of God, you may be rejected, but you are not alone. Jesus Christ himself said, *"O Jerusalem, Jerusalem, which killest the prophets, and stonest them that are sent unto thee; how often would I have gathered thy children together, as a hen doth gather her brood under her wings, and ye would not!"* (Luke 13:34). The children of Israel regularly rejected God's messengers and even the kind, parent-like care of God Himself. It is for this reason that Jesus taught His disciples that *"if the world hate you, ye know that it hated me before it hated you. If ye were of the world, the world would love his own: but because ye are not of the world, but I have chosen you out of the world, therefore the world hateth you. Remember the word that I said unto you, The servant is not greater than his lord. If they have persecuted me, they will also persecute you; if they have kept my saying, they will keep yours also. But all these things will they do unto you for my name's sake, because they know not him that sent me*" (John 15:18-21). Moses constantly faced rejection by the people of Israel as soon as things did not go their way. "*And the whole congregation of the children of Israel murmured against Moses and Aaron in the wilderness*" (Exodus 16:2). He also experienced the personal attack and rejection by fellow co-laborers and family members because of their jealousy (Numbers 12:1-3).

Paul shared his experience of rejection by some of the Corinthians believers by saying, "*And I will very gladly spend and be spent for you; though the more abundantly I love you, the less I be loved*" (I Corinthians 12:15). Paul wrote these very words to those who had rejected him personally and were attempting to discredit his ministry as an Apostle (I Corinthians 9). But Paul did not just face such rejection from the church at Corinth; he says to the church at Galatia, "*Ye know how through infirmity of the flesh I preached the gospel unto you at the first. And my temptation which was in my flesh ye despised not, nor rejected; but received me as an angel of God, even as Christ Jesus. Where is then the blessedness ye spake of? for I bear you record, that, if it had been possible, ye would have plucked out your own eyes, and have given them to me. Am I therefore become your enemy, because I tell you the truth*" (Galatians 4:13-16). Paul himself described his experience and manner of conduct during such rejections in I Corinthians 4:13 where he says, "*Being defamed, we intreat: we are made as the filth of the world, and are the offscouring of all things unto this day.*"

As a missionary follows a Biblical pattern of life and ministry, he must bear the burden of rejection with kindness and a pleading for those who have done wrong to make it right. Later in his life, King David experienced a great rejection by his nation and his companions as his son Absalom took influence over them and stole the throne from his father (II Samuel 15:1-17, 31). Such rejection of dear ones is too much too bear by oneself. Therefore you must say with David, "*As for me, I will call upon God; and the LORD shall save me. Evening, and morning, and at noon, will I pray, and cry aloud: and he shall hear my voice. He hath delivered my soul in peace from the battle that was against me: for there were many with me. God shall hear, and afflict them, even he that abideth of old. Selah. Because they have no changes, therefore they fear not God. . . . Cast thy burden upon the LORD, and he shall sustain thee: he shall never suffer the righteous to be moved. But thou, O God, shalt bring them down into the pit of destruction: bloody and deceitful men shall not live out half their days; but I will trust in thee*" (Psalm 55:17-23).

Dear servant of God, rejection cuts deep and can leave wounds that appear to be deadly. However, those wounds can heal through God's grace and Biblical love. Although there will always be scars to remind us of those devastating experiences, those scars are reminders of God's great kindness in seeing us through those rejections and healing those wounds. You must allow the scars to be formed and allow the wounds to heal completely so that they do not begin to fester with bitterness and resentment. You must learn to constantly be "*forbearing one another, and forgiving one another, if any man have a quarrel against any: even as Christ forgave you, so also do ye*" (Colossians 3:13). There must be a commitment to say with the Apostle Paul, "*And I will very gladly spend and be spent for you; though the more abundantly I love you, the less I be loved*" (II Corinthians 12:15).

Do not allow the carnality of others to distract you from sharing and displaying God's longsuffering and love for them through your daily acts of kindness (I Peter 3:9). "*For this is thankworthy, if a man for conscience toward God endure grief, suffering wrongfully. For what glory is it, if, when ye be buffeted for your faults, ye shall take it patiently? but if, when ye do well, and suffer for it, ye take it patiently, this is acceptable with God. For even hereunto were ye called: because Christ also suffered for us, leaving us an example, that ye should follow his steps: Who did no sin, neither was guile found in his mouth: Who, when he was reviled, reviled not again; when he suffered, he threatened not; but committed himself to him that judgeth righteously*" (I Peter 2:19-23). "*But and if ye suffer for righteousness' sake, happy are ye: and be not afraid of their terror, neither be troubled; but sanctify the Lord God in your hearts: and be ready always to give an answer to every man that asketh you a reason of the hope that is in you with meekness and fear: having a good conscience; that, whereas they speak evil of you, as of evildoers, they may be ashamed that falsely accuse your good conversation in Christ. For it is better, if the will of God be so, that ye suffer for well doing, than for evil doing"* (I Peter 3:14-17). *"If ye be reproached for the name of Christ, happy are ye; for the spirit of glory and of God resteth upon you: on their part he is evil spoken of, but on your part he is glorified. Yet if any man suffer as a Christian, let him not be ashamed; but let him glorify God on this behalf"* (I Peter 4:14, 16).

Actual Events

As I arrived in my field of service, the Lord provided a man who was interested in ministry training and who was able to communicate with me in my own language. This man quickly became someone I looked forward to spending time with and sharing my thoughts with. Unfortunately, due to some conflicts in the ministry which arose, coupled with an unwillingness to resolve simple sins, this man left the church and took several people with him, including two teenage boys with whom I had been spending hours each week in discipleship and ministry opportunities. This experience was very disappointing, and though the temptation came to never again share myself with another individual, God quickly reminded me that it is often through the sacrificial giving of myself and my forgiveness that other people can truly see His love through me. So as other opportunities arose I took them, cautiously of course, but willingly. Time after time, disappointments have come. Thankfully, not all of them have been due to sin or personal rejection but rather the simple need for one or the other of us to obey the Lord's leading in another direction. However, those rejections that have been more personal and even accompanied by attack have again reminded me of my commitment to *"very gladly spend and be spent for you [others]; though the more abundantly I love you [them], the less I be loved"* (II Corinthians 12:15).

Biblical Exhortation

Dear servant of God, Jesus Christ did not promise fame and friends to those who followed Him but rather, *"The servant is not greater than his lord. If they have persecuted me, they will also persecute you; if they have kept my saying, they will keep yours also"* (John 15:20). You have been called to be *"the light of the world"* (Matthew 5:14). But that does not mean that the world will appreciate you, because *"men loved darkness rather than light, because their deeds were evil. For every one that doeth evil hateth the light, neither cometh to the light, lest his deeds should be reproved* (John 3:19-20). You will have those who will reject you, your sacrifice, and your teaching just as Judas Iscariot did to Jesus Christ. But that should not distract you for your calling to be their *"servants for Jesus' sake"* (II Corinthians 4:5).

Practical Participation

✎ Missionary Candidate - Please prepare for those doubt-filled darts of Satan that will come at you as you seek to obey God. Please know that many of these doubts are simply well-meaning expressions of concern from those who love you and believe they are seeking what is best for your life and safety. Do not become discouraged, but rather turn to God more earnestly to truly know His will and strength through the knowledge of and obedience to His Word.

✎ Missionary's Supporter - Please pray for the prospective missionary as he interacts with those who may discourage him from fulfilling God's will for his life. Pray that he will constantly be reminded of God's presence and power to fulfill each and every part of God's will for his life, no matter what the price. **Please provide** him with encouraging words of Scripture and godly counsel as he seeks to evaluate the criticisms and concerns he receives. Provide him with a constant assurance of your support as he seeks to obey God no matter the consequences.

✎ Missionary in Service - Please press on. Do not allow the present or past doubts of others distract you from the perfect will of God for your life. Look to God for His counsel, and trust Him to be the supplier of every need. Be assured that no matter what you may face, you are always safest and most blessed as you stay in the center of God's will.

Increase Your Faith

Genesis 50:19-20

19 And Joseph said unto them,
Fear not: for am I in the place of God?
20 But as for you, ye thought evil against me;
but God meant it unto good, to bring to pass,
as it is this day, to save much people alive.

Luke 6:27-31

27 But I say unto you which hear,
Love your enemies, do good to them which hate you,
28 Bless them that curse you,
and pray for them which despitefully use you.
29 And unto him that smiteth thee on the one cheek
offer also the other;
and him that taketh away thy cloke
forbid not to take thy coat also.
30 Give to every man that asketh of thee;
and of him that taketh away thy goods ask them not again.
31 And as ye would that men should do to you,
do ye also to them likewise.

John 15:18-21

18 If the world hate you,
ye know that it hated me before it hated you.
19 If ye were of the world, the world would love his own:
but because ye are not of the world,
but I have chosen you out of the world,
therefore the world hateth you.
20 Remember the word that I said unto you,
The servant is not greater than his lord.
If they have persecuted me, they will also persecute you;
if they have kept my saying, they will keep yours also.

Romans 12:17-21

17 Recompense to no man evil for evil.
Provide things honest in the sight of all men.
18 If it be possible, as much as lieth in you,
live peaceably with all men.
19 Dearly beloved, avenge not yourselves,
but rather give place unto wrath:
for it is written,
Vengeance is mine; I will repay, saith the Lord.
20 Therefore if thine enemy hunger, feed him;
if he thirst, give him drink:
for in so doing thou shalt heap coals of fire on his head.
21 Be not overcome of evil, but overcome evil with good.

II Corinthians 4:5

5 For we preach not ourselves, but Christ Jesus the Lord;
and ourselves your servants for Jesus' sake.

I Peter 2:19-23

19 For this is thankworthy,
if a man for conscience toward God endure grief,
suffering wrongfully.
20 For what glory is it, if,
when ye be buffeted for your faults,
ye shall take it patiently?
but if, when ye do well, and suffer for it, ye take it patiently,
this is acceptable with God.
21 For even hereunto were ye called:
because Christ also suffered for us,
leaving us an example, that ye should follow his steps:
22 Who did no sin, neither was guile found in his mouth:
23 Who, when he was reviled, reviled not again;
when he suffered, he threatened not;
but committed himself to him that judgeth righteously:

I Peter 3:9

9 Not rendering evil for evil, or railing for railing:
but contrariwise blessing;
knowing that ye are thereunto called,
that ye should inherit a blessing.

I John 2:19

19 They went out from us, but they were not of us;
for if they had been of us,
they would no doubt have continued with us:
but they went out,
that they might be made manifest that they were not all of us.

Romans 10:17
So then faith cometh by hearing,
and hearing by the word of God.

Examples of Like Faith

Joseph/His Brothers
Genesis 37:1-36, 50:19-20

Moses/People of Israel
Exodus 15:22-24, 16:2-3, 17:1-3,
Numbers 14:1-4, 16:13-14, 41, 17:12-13, 21:4-5

Jonathan/King Saul
I Samuel 20:27-34

Jesus/Jerusalem
Luke 13:34

Jesus/Judas Iscariot
Matthew 26:48-50
Mark 14:44-46
Luke 22:47-28

Romans 15:4
For whatsoever things were written aforetime
were written for our learning,
that we through patience and comfort of the scriptures
might have hope.

Chapter 18

VANITY OF LABOR

Isaiah 49:4
Then I said, I have laboured in vain,
I have spent my strength for nought, and in vain:
yet surely my judgment is with the LORD,
and my work with my God.

The Missionary's Experience

After a few months and years of ministry, the missionary will naturally begin to evaluate his results. He will be driven to do so by the natural desire to validate his efforts and sacrifices, as well as the need to provide adequate accountability to his supporters for their generosity and participation in his life and ministry. However, he will most likely find his evaluations fall short of what his goals were when he first began. His goals had been high because he had expected that, if God had called him to minister to a specific people, He would have first made sure that those same people would be ready and willing to receive the Gospel and live according to their new life. Before leaving for the field, his supporters had joined with him in his great expectations and continually stated that they were expecting God to do great things through his life and ministry. Yet the progress he has seen has been slow. The days of sowing have been long and he has begun to feel as though no matter his efforts, there is a spiritual drought that no one could overcome. He has found that his efforts for evangelism have fallen on deaf ears and those few professing Christians who claim to have new lives in Christ continue to live in the sin of their old lives as they refuse to personally and practically apply his preaching and teaching of God's Word. He has sacrificed all to lovingly and endlessly labor in sharing God's Word and His love with strangers, and yet he is deeply saddened to find that all he has worked for and all he sacrificed for has come to vanity, as those around him have refused to apply and practice his teaching.

Biblical Examples

Dear servant of God, do not believe that, although you are to *"be ye stedfast, unmoveable, always abounding in the work of the Lord, forasmuch as ye know that your labour is not in vain in the Lord,"* your labor will not be in vain with man (I Corinthians 15:58). The Apostle Paul was concerned that his ministry of preaching the Gospel to the people of Corinth was in vain because they may have *"believed in vain"* (I Corinthians 15:2). While writing to the church in Galatia, he specifically said, *"I am afraid of you, lest I have bestowed upon you labour in vain"* (Galatians 4:11). Paul was deeply concerned about the vanity of his labor, because the believers were returning to their old lives and beliefs after he had instructed them in the truths of the Gospel. And although Paul confidently stated that his labor in Thessalonica *"was not in vain"* (I Thessalonians 2:1), he later shared his concern that Satan had destroyed his labor, and so he *"sent to know your [their] faith, lest by some means the tempter have tempted you [them], and our labour be in vain"* (I Thessalonians 3:5). Vanity and wastefulness in ministry result not because the minister does not receive rewards from God, but because the people who are receiving the ministry do not take heed to it and live in accordance with it. They have wasted the opportunity to live changed lives, and therefore the loving and sacrificial efforts of the minister are of no value in their lives.

The prophet Jeremiah expressed his frustration at the vanity of his ministry by saying, *"O LORD, thou hast deceived me, and I was deceived: thou art stronger than I, and hast prevailed: I am in derision daily, every one mocketh me. For since I spake, I cried out, I cried violence and spoil; because the word of the LORD was made a reproach unto me, and a derision, daily"* (Jeremiah 20:7-8). Jeremiah accepted God's creative purpose and call for his life as God declared to him, *"Before I formed thee in the belly I knew thee; and before thou camest forth out of the womb I sanctified thee, and I ordained thee a prophet unto the nations"* (Jeremiah 1:5). And he experienced the touch of God's hand upon his mouth as He promised him, *"Behold, I have put my words in thy mouth. See, I have this day set thee over the nations and over the kingdoms, to root out, and to pull down, and to destroy, and to throw down, to build, and to plant"* (Jeremiah 1:9-10). But after years of being ignored and having his message rejected, he grew frustrated and found no human reason to keep preaching and said, *"I will not make mention of him, nor speak any more in his name. But his word was in mine heart as a burning fire shut up in my bones, and I was weary with forbearing, and I could not stay"* (Jeremiah 20:9). The reality of vanity in ministry is one of the largest burdens ever born by a minister. He is often willing to nobly sacrifice as long as his message is being listened to and heeded. But when he realizes that his words have been wasted upon the people who do not care, he will often join Jeremiah in saying that "enough is enough," until the burning need to share God's Word grows more powerful than the lack of interest by the hearers. This vanity in labor is perhaps best stated in Isaiah 49:4, which begins, *"Then I said, I have laboured in vain, I have spent my strength for nought, and in vain."* But the servant of God does not end with this thought, but rather he continues to find true value in ministry as he concludes, *"Yet surely my judgment is with the LORD, and my work with my God"* (Isaiah 49:4).

Actual Events

My ministry is no different from these examples from scripture. Before leaving for my field of service, the hopes of my supporters were high. Comments like, "I am sure you will make a great impact in your new ministry" surrounded me as people continually encouraged me to obey God's call for my life. Even as I arrived on my field of service and first began to minister, the people's interest in a new message and messenger provided a platform for ministry. But, sadly, the excitement subsided, and those who had declared their commitment to God's Word faded; and many of those who chose to stay became inoculated to the power of the Word of God as Satan, the world, and their flesh began to cause distractions and provided excuses for disobedience to the clear message of God's Word. Months of *"serving the Lord with all humility of mind, and with many tears, and temptations"* turned into years (Acts 20:19). And as we continued to keep *"back nothing that was profitable unto you [them], but have shewed you [them], and have taught you [them] publickly, and from house to house, testifying . . . repentance toward God, and faith toward our Lord Jesus Christ,"* the indifference to obedience seemed to grow (Acts 20:20-21). How exhausting and discouraging this reality has become to me as I watch those whom I have loved sow to the flesh and reap the corruption that follows, all the while knowing that if each one would simply stop being a *"forgetful hearer, but a doer of the work"* they would be blessed in their deeds (James 1:25). The vanity of ministry has caused occasion for personal evaluation of my personal weaknesses in ministry; it has provided at times a desire to *"shake off the very dust from your [my] feet for a testimony against them,"* perhaps before God's timing to do so is revealed (Luke 9:5). And yet, as I have received the strength of God to continue based upon His faithfulness, I depend more and more upon His *"mercy"* so that I will *"faint not"* while remembering that *"if our gospel be hid, it is hid to them that are lost: in whom the god of this world hath blinded the minds of them which believe not, lest the light of the glorious gospel of Christ, who is the image of God, should shine unto them"* (II Corinthians 4:1-5).

Biblical Exhortation

Dear servant of God, *"be ye stedfast, unmoveable, always abounding in the work of the Lord, forasmuch as ye know that your labour is not in vain in the Lord,"* always remembering that God has promised, *"So shall my word be that goeth forth out of my mouth: it shall not return unto me void, but it shall accomplish that which I please, and it shall prosper in the thing whereto I sent it*" (I Corinthians 15:58, Isaiah 55:11). Take the time to carefully and prayerfully evaluate your life and ministry to make sure that you are a *"vessel unto honour, sanctified and meet for the master's use, and prepared unto every good work*" and that you are not the cause of vanity in your ministry (II Timothy 2:21). And then, understand that it is not your responsibility to produce spiritual fruit, but rather plant and sow the seed of God's Word while understanding that it is *"God that giveth the increase*" (I Corinthians 3:7). Recognize that your life and ministry is full of purpose as you follow the example of King Solomon when he said, *"And moreover, because the preacher was wise, he still taught the people knowledge; yea, he gave good heed, and sought out, and set in order many proverbs. The preacher sought to find out acceptable words: and that which was written was upright, even words of truth*" (Ecclesiastes 12:9-10). And he concludes his words of truth by saying, *"Let us hear the conclusion of the whole matter: Fear God, and keep his commandments: for this is the whole duty of man. For God shall bring every work into judgment, with every secret thing, whether it be good, or whether it be evil*" (Ecclesiastes 12:13-14). Set your ministry goals upon warning those who will listen, as Paul taught by saying, *"Do all things without murmurings and disputings: that ye may be blameless and harmless, the sons of God, without rebuke, in the midst of a crooked and perverse nation, among whom ye shine as lights in the world; holding forth the word of life; that I may rejoice in the day of Christ, that I have not run in vain, neither laboured in vain*" (Philippians 2:14-16).

Practical Participation

Missionary Candidate - Please prepare your heart for the reality that your best efforts cannot change the heart of man and that your sacrifice, although an offering of great value to God, may not be counted valuable to those you seek to reach. As you prepare to depart for life-long service, recognize that success or failure, value or vanity, do not rest with men but with God. Be confident of God's call without placing qualifications upon your obedience to faithfulness.

Missionary's Supporter - Please pray for your missionary as he watches those he has sacrificed for reject his preaching and teaching. Pray for him to be filled with the love of Christ to continue in a proper love for those who have become indifferent to their spiritual needs and expectant to his sacrifice. **Please provide** him with words of encouragement rather than disappointment when times are tough and human results are not being realized. And be careful to not be judgmental of him because of a lack of results, based upon the knowledge that the he is only called to faithfulness and not success.

Missionary in Service - Please press on by accepting the reality of the possibility of "vanity" in ministry. Realize that others have served all of their lives and have never seen the fruit of their labor because they were planting and sowing so that God could produce a harvest for the next generation. Recognize that human success may win temporal approval, but personal faithfulness will gain eternal reward. Do not ever give up on the call of God on your ministry nor forget the promises of God for your life.

Increase Your Faith

Isaiah 49:1-6

1 Listen, O isles, unto me;
and hearken, ye people, from far;
The LORD hath called me from the womb;
from the bowels of my mother
hath he made mention of my name.
2 And he hath made my mouth like a sharp sword;
in the shadow of his hand hath he hid me,
and made me a polished shaft;
in his quiver hath he hid me;
3 And said unto me, Thou art my servant, O Israel,
in whom I will be glorified.
4 Then I said, I have laboured in vain,
I have spent my strength for nought, and in vain:
yet surely my judgment is with the LORD,
and my work with my God.
5 And now, saith the LORD that formed me
from the womb to be his servant,
to bring Jacob again to him,
Though Israel be not gathered,
yet shall I be glorious in the eyes of the LORD,
and my God shall be my strength.
6 And he said, It is a light thing
that thou shouldest be my servant
to raise up the tribes of Jacob,
and to restore the preserved of Israel:
I will also give thee for a light to the Gentiles,
that thou mayest be my salvation
unto the end of the earth.

Isaiah 55:11
11 So shall my word be that goeth forth out of my mouth:
it shall not return unto me void,
but it shall accomplish that which I please,
and it shall prosper in the thing whereto I sent it.

Psalm 126:5-6
5 They that sow in tears shall reap in joy.
6 He that goeth forth and weepeth,
bearing precious seed,
shall doubtless come again with rejoicing,
bringing his sheaves with him.

Psalm 127:1
1 Except the LORD build the house,
they labour in vain that build it:
except the LORD keep the city,
the watchman waketh but in vain.

John 4:35-38
35 Say not ye,
There are yet four months, and then cometh harvest?
behold, I say unto you,
Lift up your eyes, and look on the fields;
for they are white already to harvest.
36 And he that reapeth receiveth wages,
and gathereth fruit unto life eternal:
that both he that soweth and he that reapeth
may rejoice together.
37 And herein is that saying true,
One soweth, and another reapeth.
38 I sent you to reap
that whereon ye bestowed no labour:
other men laboured,
and ye are entered into their labours.

I Corinthians 3:5-9

5 Who then is Paul, and who is Apollos,
but ministers by whom ye believed,
even as the Lord gave to every man?
6 I have planted, Apollos watered;
but God gave the increase.
7 So then neither is he that planteth any thing,
neither he that watereth;
but God that giveth the increase.
8 Now he that planteth and he that watereth are one:
and every man shall receive his own reward
according to his own labour.
9 For we are labourers together with God:
ye are God's husbandry, ye are God's building.

Galatians 6:9

9 And let us not be weary in well doing:
for in due season we shall reap, if we faint not.

Ephesians 6:8

8 Knowing that whatsoever good thing any man doeth,
the same shall he receive of the Lord,
whether he be bond or free.

Philippians 2:14-16

14 Do all things without murmurings and disputings:
15 That ye may be blameless and harmless,
the sons of God, without rebuke,
in the midst of a crooked and perverse nation,
among whom ye shine as lights in the world;
16 Holding forth the word of life;
that I may rejoice in the day of Christ,
that I have not run in vain, neither laboured in vain.

Colossians 2:8, 18
8 *Beware lest any man spoil you*
through philosophy and vain deceit,
after the tradition of men,
after the rudiments of the world,
and not after Christ.
18 *Let no man beguile you*
of your reward in a voluntary humility
and worshipping of angels,
intruding into those things which he hath not seen,
vainly puffed up by his fleshly mind,

Hebrews 6:10
10 *For God is not unrighteous*
to forget your work and labour of love,
which ye have shewed toward his name,
in that ye have ministered to the saints, and do minister.

Romans 10:17
So then faith cometh by hearing,
and hearing by the word of God.

Examples of Like Faith

God
Genesis 4:1-16

Moses
Exodus 4:1-12:51

Jesus Christ
John 10:23-30

Stephen
Acts 6:8-7:60

Romans 15:4
For whatsoever things were written aforetime
were written for our learning,
that we through patience and comfort of the scriptures
might have hope.

Chapter 19

BITTER FAILURES

Philippians 3:13-14
*Brethren, I count not myself to have apprehended:
but this one thing I do,
forgetting those things which are behind,
and reaching forth unto those things which are before,
I press toward the mark for the prize of the high calling of God
in Christ Jesus.*

The Missionary's Experience

The missionary's arrival on his field of service is full of possibilities, expectations, and dreams. He has arrived to his new home for the single purpose of displaying his love for his Savior by being His ambassador to share the message of salvation with those who have never heard. But some of these possibilities, expectations, and dreams may quickly seem to become unattainable due to his inability in the language, lack of understanding of the culture, etc. He has sacrificed all to share the Gospel but fails in being able to present it clearly. He has asked his family to join him in his adventure, but he is helpless to truly assure them the provision and protection they need. He may begin to see himself as a presenter of big ideas in his home country but an utter failure as a husband, father, and minister in his new land. Thankfully, this initial sense of bitter failure begins to fade away as he adjusts to his new environment and is able to get his family settled and his ministry started. As he becomes usefully involved in the ministry, he begins to once again consider some new possibilities, expectations, and dreams for the future. These new plans may be similar to those he had when he first arrived on the field, but now they are tempered by his experiences and the understanding he has gained about the realities of life and ministry in his new circumstances.

Now the missionary will face two other types of failures that every spiritual leader faces as he seeks to serve God with all his heart and serve others with all his life. The first type of failure he will face is that of his own sin. Although the missionary is supposed to be "spiritual," the temptations he faces and the weakness of his own flesh will bring him to say with the Apostle Paul, "*For we know that the law is spiritual: but I am carnal, sold under sin. For that which I do I allow not: for what I would, that do I not; but what I hate, that do I. If then I do that which I would not, I consent unto the law that it is good. Now then it is no more I that do it, but sin that dwelleth in me. For I know that in me (that is, in my flesh,) dwelleth no good thing: for to will is present with me; but how to perform that which is good I find not. For the good that I would I do not: but the evil which I would not, that I do. Now if I do that I would not, it is no more I that do it, but sin that dwelleth in me. I find then a law, that, when I would do good, evil is present with me. For I delight in the law of God after the inward man: But I see another law in my members, warring against the law of my mind, and bringing me into captivity to the law of sin which is in my members. O wretched man that I am! who shall deliver me from the body of this death? I thank God through Jesus Christ our Lord. So then with the mind I myself serve the law of God; but with the flesh the law of sin*" (Romans 7:14-25). The missionary has dedicated his life to serve a holy God but fights daily with his own flesh in order to not violate God's standard of holiness: "*Be ye holy; for I am holy*" (I Peter 1:16). As the missionary fails in his personal holiness, he must face the bitter reality that his sins affect both his family and ministry. If the missionary is not careful to quickly recognize his failure of sin and humbly deal with its results, the damages could be irreversible.

The last type of failure the missionary faces includes situations and circumstance outside of his control but that prevent him from caring for those dear to him in the way he would like. These failures are not necessarily the missionary's fault (health, traffic, etc.), but he will often still experience the bitterness of failure as he is unable to protect and provide for those around him. He will be faced with the constant question of "what if . . .," which is beneficial as a learning opportunity, but detrimental if it causes continual self-doubt and frustration with God for not changing the circumstance more favorably. All in all, the missionary will look at all unrealized expectations, possibilities, and dreams as failures: failures that are taken personally and hurt him deeply. Whether large or small, Satan will try to use these failures against him to discourage him and send him home long before it is God's time.

Biblical Examples

Dear servant of God, unrealized expectations and personal failures can become some of the greatest burdens you will bear. These burdens can hold you back, or you can turn them back over to God and ask Him to mature you through them. Peter faced such a decision. While in the upper room, Jesus said to Peter, "***Simon, Simon, behold, Satan hath desired to have you, that he may sift you as wheat: But I have prayed for thee, that thy faith fail not: and when thou art converted, strengthen thy brethren***" (Luke 22:31-32). Peter responded to Jesus in sincere dedication by declaring his personal expectations for himself as he said, "***Lord, I am ready to go with thee, both into prison, and to death***" (Luke 22:33). Peter had walked with Jesus for three years and had enjoyed being part of His inner circle. He had been with Jesus when He performed His miracles and preached in the temple against the Jewish leaders. He watched Jesus calm the sea and had obeyed His command to walk to Him on water. The very idea that Peter would now fail Jesus was unthinkable. But Jesus knew the amount of pressure Satan would bring on Peter, and He warned him and prayed for him. Sadly, Peter's dedication waned, and he denied Jesus Christ three times (Luke 22:54-60). "***And the Lord turned, and looked upon Peter. And Peter remembered the word of the Lord, how he had said*** *unto him, Before the cock crow, thou shalt deny me thrice. And Peter went out, and wept bitterly*" (Luke 22:61-62). The bitterness of Peter's failure to his Lord was devastating and led him to believe that his work for God was over. Just three years earlier, Jesus had said to Him, "*Follow me, and I will make you fishers of men*" (Matthew 4:19). Peter immediately followed his call, but after this failure, he believed his calling to be worthless and his life to have no more ministry purpose; so he said to the other disciples "*I go a fishing*" (John 21:3). When Jesus had warned Peter of Satan's attack and his imminent failure, He said, "*But I have prayed for thee, that thy faith fail not: and when thou art converted, strengthen thy brethren*" (Luke 22:32). Jesus Christ knew that Peter's faith would wane but that it would not completely fail. He wanted Peter to know that the bitterness of failure did not need to destroy him but that he could change the direction of his life and be restored in his personal relationship and purpose of ministry. Peter's failure gave him the opportunity to understand more fully his need to depend on God as well as help others in their time of Satanic attack. Peter's relationship with Jesus was restored, and he was given the extreme privilege of being mightily used of God on the day of Pentecost as the keynote preacher, as well as throughout the rest of the establishment of the early church (John 21:1-19, Acts 2:1-47).

Paul also faced personal failures and disappointments. He desired to personally minister to the believers in Rome but was only able to write a letter to say, "*For God is my witness, whom I serve with my spirit in the gospel of his Son, that without ceasing I make mention of you always in my prayers; making request, if by any means now at length I might have a prosperous journey by the will of God to come unto you. For I long to see you, that I may impart unto you some spiritual gift, to the end ye may be established; that is, that I may be comforted together with you by the mutual faith both of you and me. Now I would not have you ignorant, brethren, that oftentimes I purposed to come unto you, (but was let hitherto,) that I might have some fruit among you also, even as among other Gentiles.*" (Romans 1:9-12, 15:22). He said to them, "*Now I would not have you ignorant, brethren, that oftentimes I purposed to come unto you, (but was let hitherto,)*" (Romans 1:13). Paul was clear—his purpose for being with them was so he could minister to them, but his human efforts were hindered by circumstances outside of his control. Paul's desire to minister to believers was sincere, and his efforts real, but he failed to fulfill his goal. Paul, while speaking to the church at Thessalonica, spoke of another ministry failure when he said, "*But we, brethren, being taken from you for a short time in presence, not in heart, endeavoured the more abundantly to see your face with great desire. Wherefore we would have come unto you, even I Paul, once and again; but Satan hindered us*" (I Thessalonians 2:17-18). On this occasion, Paul did not believe his general circumstances were to blame for this failure to minister but rather the specific influence and manipulation of Satan himself. Paul was a passionate minister. He had a passion for people, to be with people, and to serve people. When he was unable to fulfill his passion, he felt the bitterness of disappointment, but Paul did not allow these hindrances to prevent him from trying "*once and again*" (I Thessalonians 2:18).

Actual Events

Throughout my life I have failed myself and others on many occasions. I have taken these failures very personally and seriously. I believe that there is no excuse for sin or for any failure in fulfilling my responsibilities to my utmost ability. One of my most memorable failures in ministry can be partially attributed to misinformation as well as a lack of discernment to see past that information (Joshua 9:3-27, Nehemiah 6:1-13). That failure took its toll on me personally within my first year of full-time ministry. The bitterness of that situation included the opportunity for others to question and attack my integrity, my sincerity for God, and my dedication to those to whom I was ministering. Although their attacks were proven to be invalid as time passed, the very thought that I had given them the slightest opportunity to slander God's ministry was devastating. I thank God for fellow believers and ministers who counseled and encouraged me during this difficult time. Through the process, I learned for myself what Paul meant when he said to the believers at Corinth who doubted his ministry, "*But with me it is a very small thing that I should be judged of you, or of man's judgment: . . . but he that judgeth me is the Lord*" (I Corinthians 4:3-5).

This event did not eliminate other failures in ministry, but it did teach me an utter hatred of personal failure. Unfortunately, I still fail regularly. Just within the last few months, I failed to make it from a funeral home to the graveside service where I had been asked by an unsaved widow to share comforting words from Scripture. Those moments of watching the funeral procession weave through the unfamiliar town and then fade into the distance while I was caught at a red light were unbearable. The frantic visiting of every cemetery in the town searching for the family brought a feeling of panic and rage like I had not felt in years. I finally had to resign to end my search and return to the widow's home to wait for her to return from burying her young husband without a Gospel witness being presented publicly to her, her family, or friends. These circumstances were outside of my imagination. I had no idea that they would be going to a cemetery thirty to forty minutes away nor that they would be taking a route through some back roads to get there. Perhaps I could have been more bold in running a red light or pushing my way through the other sorrowing family members to be at the front of the line or even probed more deeply to find out the exact location of the gravesite, but none of those things seemed to be reasonable options until after I saw the procession fade away. This ministry failure will always grieve my heart, and yet I must trust that God had His purpose in allowing it.

Biblical Exhortation

Dear servant of God, failure is imminent. You must accept your failures and confess any sins that may have caused them, and you must also accept that "failures" outside of your control are not your burdens to bear. For each failure because of your sin, you must say to God as David did, *"Have mercy upon me, O God, according to thy lovingkindness: according unto the multitude of thy tender mercies blot out my transgressions. Wash me throughly from mine iniquity, and cleanse me from my sin. For I acknowledge my transgressions: and my sin is ever before me. Against thee, thee only, have I sinned, and done this evil in thy sight: that thou mightest be justified when thou speakest, and be clear when thou judgest"*

(Psalm 51:1-4). You must *"confess your faults one to another"* so as to restore any broken relationships with those around you (James 5:16). For each failure outside of your control, you must remind yourself that *"God meant it unto good,"* and realize with the Apostle Paul that a failure to minister in one area may be God's leading to minister in another (Genesis 50:20, Acts 16:6-12). Failure should push you to depend on God more, to recognize your complete inability without His almighty power. You must not continually consume yourself with the past, but must look to the future as Paul did when he said, *"Brethren, I count not myself to have apprehended: but this one thing I do, forgetting those things which are behind, and reaching forth unto those things which are before, I press toward the mark for the prize of the high calling of God in Christ Jesus"* (Philippians 3:13-14).

Practical Participation

✎ **Missionary Candidate - Please prepare** yourself by recognizing your personal failure as sin and confessing it as quickly as possible. Then, take special care to learn from your failure so that you do not repeat it. Prepare yourself by learning to accept those circumstances which are outside of your control as being in God's control. Then look for new opportunities to minister for Him wherever those circumstances lead you.

✎ **Missionary's Supporter - Please pray** for your missionary as he faces personal disappointments and failures on a regular basis. Pray that each failure would not be used by Satan to destroy the missionary or those around him but that he would quickly find God's forgiveness for personal sin. Pray that he would be able to seek God's guidance in those failures that are outside of his control, and ask God to quickly open new doors of opportunity through each "failure." **Please provide** him with gracious edification when he faces personal failures and encouraging anticipation of future ministry when there is "failure" outside of his control (Galatians 6:1).

✎ **Missionary in Service - Please press on** by first recognizing personal failure and taking it seriously. Accept the responsibility for what is truly your fault and seek God's proper restoration. Press on by seeing those "failures" outside of your control as being God's guiding hand to future ministry. Do not allow personal or uncontrolled failures to discourage you from faithfully looking to future personal spiritual growth and ministry.

Increase Your Faith

Psalm 37:23-24

23 The steps of a good man are ordered by the LORD:
and he delighteth in his way.
24 Though he fall, he shall not be utterly cast down:
for the LORD upholdeth him with his hand.

Psalm 51:1-19
(1-4, 6-7, 9-10, 12-13, 15-17)
1 Have mercy upon me, O God,
according to thy lovingkindness:
according unto the multitude of thy tender mercies
blot out my transgressions.
2 Wash me throughly from mine iniquity,
and cleanse me from my sin.
3 For I acknowledge my transgressions:
and my sin is ever before me.
4 Against thee, thee only, have I sinned,
and done this evil in thy sight:
that thou mightest be justified when thou speakest,
and be clear when thou judgest.
6 Behold, thou desirest truth in the inward parts:
and in the hidden part thou shalt make me to know wisdom.
7 Purge me with hyssop, and I shall be clean:
wash me, and I shall be whiter than snow.
9 Hide thy face from my sins,
and blot out all mine iniquities.
10 Create in me a clean heart, O God;
and renew a right spirit within me.
12 Restore unto me the joy of thy salvation;
and uphold me with thy free spirit.
13 Then will I teach transgressors thy ways;
and sinners shall be converted unto thee.

15 O Lord, open thou my lips;
and my mouth shall shew forth thy praise.
16 For thou desirest not sacrifice; else would I give it:
thou delightest not in burnt offering.
17 The sacrifices of God are a broken spirit:
a broken and a contrite heart, O God,
thou wilt not despise.

Philippians 3:12-15
12 Not as though I had already attained,
either were already perfect:
but I follow after,
if that I may apprehend that for which also
I am apprehended of Christ Jesus.
13 Brethren, I count not myself to have apprehended:
but this one thing I do,
forgetting those things which are behind,
and reaching forth unto those things which are before,
14 I press toward the mark for the prize
of the high calling of God in Christ Jesus.
15 Let us therefore, as many as be perfect, be thus minded:
and if in any thing ye be otherwise minded,
God shall reveal even this unto you.

I John 1:7-10
7 But if we walk in the light, as he is in the light,
we have fellowship one with another,
and the blood of Jesus Christ his Son
cleanseth us from all sin.
8 If we say that we have no sin, we deceive ourselves,
and the truth is not in us.
9 If we confess our sins,
he is faithful and just to forgive us our sins,
and to cleanse us from all unrighteousness.
10 If we say that we have not sinned,
we make him a liar, and his word is not in us.

I John 3:19-22

19 And hereby we know that we are of the truth,
and shall assure our hearts before him.
20 For if our heart condemn us,
God is greater than our heart, and knoweth all things.
21 Beloved, if our heart condemn us not,
then have we confidence toward God.
22 And whatsoever we ask, we receive of him,
because we keep his commandments,
and do those things that are pleasing in his sight.

Romans 10:17
So then faith cometh by hearing,
and hearing by the word of God.

Examples of Like Faith

Abraham
Genesis 12:10-20, 16:1-16, 20:1-18

Joshua
Joshua 9:1-27

David
II Samuel 11:1-24

Romans 15:4
For whatsoever things were written aforetime
were written for our learning,
that we through patience and comfort of the scriptures
might have hope.

Chapter 20

SATISFACTION WITH SUCCESS

Proverbs 16:18
*Pride goeth before destruction,
and an haughty spirit before a fall.*

The Missionary's Experience

The missionary's greatest God-given blessing can become the stumbling block for his greatest downfall. The missionary who enjoys quick success in ministry and gains early influences with those around him will face the very temptation Satan fell prey to: pride. If the missionary arrives on his field of service and quickly begins to see souls saved and churches planted, he will be tempted to believe that "he" is accomplishing a great work. If the missionary is welcomed to influential circles and given prominent positions due to his charisma, education, or ministry connection and does not accept each privilege without humbling himself before God by depending on His power and wisdom (Solomon - I Kings 3:9-14), he will face the destruction as a novice who *"being lifted up with pride he fall into the condemnation of the devil"* (I Timothy 3:6). These pressures on the missionary are not public. In fact, they are not seen as pressures at all, but as the very blessing of God and evidence of God's hand of approval on the man and his ministry. However, just as God seeks to bless those who are faithful to Him, so Satan seeks to destroy them. The temptation to be lifted up with pride because of his success will be strong, and the missionary will need to continually guard his heart. His success or failure in this matter may not be revealed quickly since the fruit may not be revealed until years after the damage has been done to his family and personal testimony. He must be constantly on guard because *"pride goeth before destruction, and an haughty spirit before a fall"* (Proverbs 16:18).

Biblical Examples

Dear servant of God, you must be on guard at all times. Many great men of God, who have experienced great blessing, have failed in the end because they did not maintain a humble spirit. They began to believe that their success was of their own doing. King Saul was a *"choice young man, and a goodly: and there was not among the children of Israel a goodlier person than he: from his shoulders and upward he was higher than any of the people"* (I Samuel 9:2), but after leading for a time and building a kingdom (ministry), he began to consider himself to be a self-made king. So Samuel confronted him with this harsh reality by saying, *"When thou wast little in thine own sight, wast thou not made the head of the tribes of Israel, and the LORD anointed thee king over Israel? . . . Because thou hast rejected the word of the LORD, he hath also rejected thee from being king"* (I Samuel 15:17). King Saul's reign began in humility but was destroyed by his pride. The defeat of success is not seen immediately, but it is imminent; for *"God resisteth the proud, but giveth grace unto the humble"* (James 4:6), and *"pride goeth before destruction, and an haughty spirit before a fall"* (Proverbs 16:18).

King Nebuchadnezzar also faced a time of great humiliation because of his pride. King Nebuchadnezzar, as the king of Babylon, established a great kingdom that included Judah, which *"the Lord gave . . . into his hand"* (Daniel 1:1-2). As he placed Jews throughout his administration and kingdom, he was introduced to the only true God of Daniel and Shadrach, Meshach, and Abednego (Daniel 1-3). In spite of that, he became lifted up with pride *"and said, Is not this great Babylon, that I have built for the house of the kingdom by the might of my power, and for the honour of my majesty?"* (Daniel 4:30). God said to him from heaven, *"O king Nebuchadnezzar, to thee it is spoken; The kingdom is departed from thee. And they shall drive thee from men, and thy dwelling shall be with the beasts of the field: they shall make thee to eat grass as oxen, and seven times shall pass over thee, until thou know that the most High ruleth in the kingdom of men, and giveth it to whomsoever he will. The same hour was the thing fulfilled upon Nebuchadnezzar: and he was driven from men, and did eat grass as oxen, and his body was wet with the dew of heaven, till his hairs were grown like eagles' feathers, and his nails like birds' claws"* (Daniel 4:31-33). Following God's punishment of his pride, King Nebuchadnezzar returned to his senses and declares his personal transformation by saying, *"I Nebuchadnezzar lifted up mine eyes unto heaven, and mine understanding returned unto me, and I blessed the most High, and I praised and honoured him that liveth for ever, whose dominion is an everlasting dominion, and his kingdom is from generation to generation: And all the inhabitants of the earth are reputed as nothing: and he doeth according to his will in the army of heaven, and among the inhabitants of the earth: and none can stay his hand, or say unto him, What doest thou? At the same time my reason returned unto me; and for the glory of my kingdom, mine honour and brightness returned unto me; and my counsellors and my lords sought unto me; and I was established in my kingdom, and excellent majesty was added unto me. Now I Nebuchadnezzar praise and extol and honour the King of heaven, all whose works are truth, and his ways judgment: and those that walk in pride he is able to abase"* (Daniel 4:34-37). God was gracious to King Nebuchadnezzar, as He allowed him to once again return to his kingdom and his throne, but only after his heart was changed from looking at himself to looking to *"the most High."*

Actual Events

Neither my life nor my ministry has ever been one of instant success or grand victories. As a student in school, I needed to work hard for the grades I brought home. As an athlete, I rarely enjoyed the privilege of playing for banner-winning teams. In ministry, the joy of success has been seen through little victories rather than great conquests. However, I have realized the need to humble myself after each small success so that I might continue to see God's hand of blessing throughout my future. Unfortunately, I have witnessed those in ministry who have found success and believed that it came through their efforts, a specific process, and a set time-span. Sadly, although one missionary established one solid and well-grounded ministry (his first one), those ministries that he started later were weak, and some even failed a short time after he left. But, when you talked to him, he would make reference to his first success, claim he had taken the same care in his other ministries, and never recognize the failures he had made. This self-satisfaction led to several ministries being started, but almost none of them were truly grounded so that they could become self-supporting and self-propagating for future generations. I praise God for this man's example in his first ministry, but I have learned to be careful with personal satisfaction as I endeavor to be a success for God throughout my entire ministry.

Biblical Exhortation

Dear servant of God, quick success in ministry is not quick success at all. The success that one minister enjoys is often the result of God's working hand and another minister's sacrifice for years before the "successful" minister arrived on the scene. The new missionary, who finds the fields are *"white already to harvest,"* must consider the years of preparation taken to prepare the soil and plant and water the seed. Often, when there is a quick harvest for one man, he has had the privilege of going where God has already done a great work and where *"other men laboured, and ye [they] are entered into their labours"* (John 4:35, 38). Therefore, the blessed missionary who finds people hungry for the Gospel must recognize his need to depend on God to continue the work that has already been begun. He must see himself as only a small part of the larger process. *"For we are labourers together with God"* (I Corinthians 3:9). *"So then neither is he that planteth any thing, neither he that watereth; but God that giveth the increase. Now he that planteth and he that watereth are one: and every man shall receive his own reward according to his own labour*" (I Corinthians 3:7-8). Whether you enjoy fast or slow success, you must always remember that success can be short-lived if you do not maintain a humble heart. You must be sure to always give God the glory, because it is "*God that gave the increase*" (I Corinthians 3:6).

Practical Participation

✎ **Missionary Candidate - Please prepare** your heart for future success by accepting each present success with humility and proper praise to God. Prepare yourself by doing specific studies of successful servants of God and pay special attention to their success or failure in staying humble until the end.

✎ **Missionary's Supporter - Please pray** for your missionary as he begins to see results in ministry. Pray that he will always recognize that God is the producer of each success and therefore deserves all the glory. **Please provide** him with limited personal praise. Share words of praise to God for making use of his servant and blessing his servant's efforts.

✎ **Missionary in Service - Please press on** by being honest about your inability to produce any success by publicly and privately admitting that it is by God's grace that each accomplishment is realized. Press on being useful to God in His ministry by removing any self-praise or self-dependence.

Increase Your Faith

I Samuel 15:22-23
22 And Samuel said,
Hath the LORD as great delight
in burnt offerings and sacrifices,
as in obeying the voice of the LORD?
Behold, to obey is better than sacrifice,
and to hearken than the fat of rams.
23 For rebellion is as the sin of witchcraft,
and stubbornness is as iniquity and idolatry.
Because thou hast rejected the word of the LORD,
he hath also rejected thee from being king.

Proverbs 11:2
2 When pride cometh, then cometh shame:
but with the lowly is wisdom.

Proverbs 16:18-20
18 Pride goeth before destruction,
and an haughty spirit before a fall.
19 Better it is to be of an humble spirit with the lowly,
than to divide the spoil with the proud.
20 He that handleth a matter wisely shall find good:
and whoso trusteth in the LORD, happy is he.

John 4:35-38

35 Say not ye, There are yet four months,
and then cometh harvest?
behold, I say unto you,
Lift up your eyes, and look on the fields;
for they are white already to harvest.
36 And he that reapeth receiveth wages,
and gathereth fruit unto life eternal:
that both he that soweth and he that reapeth
may rejoice together.
37 And herein is that saying true,
One soweth, and another reapeth.
38 I sent you to reap
that whereon ye bestowed no labour:
other men laboured,
and ye are entered into their labours.

I Corinthians 3:4-8

4 For while one saith, I am of Paul;
and another, I am of Apollos;
are ye not carnal?
5 Who then is Paul, and who is Apollos,
but ministers by whom ye believed,
even as the Lord gave to every man?
6 I have planted, Apollos watered;
but God gave the increase.
7 So then neither is he that planteth any thing,
neither he that watereth;
but God that giveth the increase.
8 Now he that planteth and he that watereth are one:
and every man shall receive his own reward
according to his own labour.

I Corinthians 4:6-7

6 And these things, brethren,
I have in a figure transferred to myself
and to Apollos for your sakes;
that ye might learn in us
not to think of men above that which is written,
that no one of you be puffed up
for one against another.
7 For who maketh thee to differ from another?
and what hast thou that thou didst not receive?
now if thou didst receive it, why dost thou glory,
as if thou hadst not received it?

II Corinthians 10:12-13

12 For we dare not make ourselves of the number,
or compare ourselves with some that commend themselves:
but they measuring themselves by themselves,
and comparing themselves among themselves, are not wise.
13 But we will not boast of things without our measure,
but according to the measure of the rule
which God hath distributed to us,
a measure to reach even unto you.

James 4:5-6

5 Do ye think that the scripture saith in vain,
The spirit that dwelleth in us lusteth to envy?
6 But he giveth more grace. Wherefore he saith,
God resisteth the proud,
but giveth grace unto the humble.

Romans 10:17
So then faith cometh by hearing,
and hearing by the word of God.

Examples of Like Faith

Herod
Acts 14:21-23

Paul
Acts 14:11-18, 28:1-6

Romans 15:4
For whatsoever things were written aforetime
were written for our learning,
that we through patience and comfort of the scriptures
might have hope.

www.ingramcontent.com/pod-product-compliance
Lightning Source LLC
LaVergne TN
LVHW051626080426
835511LV00016B/2191